FROM THE BOOKS OF
Mollie Lee Pryor

MR. NIXON

AND MY OTHER PROBLEMS

With much love, and good reading. to Mollie Lee

from

grandma

Dec 25th 1971

MR. NIXON

AND MY OTHER PROBLEMS

by arthur hoppe

Chronicle Books San Francisco

To Richard M. Nixon
for his help over the years

Library of Congress Catalog No. 73-171452

ISBN Prefix 0-87701-071-10

Contents

1 MR. NIXON

MY OTHER PROBLEMS

2 The Environment and Other Disaster Areas

3 Modern Living and Who Needs It?

4 The Generation Gap and Let's Keep It That Way

5 All Men Are Brothers and They Fight Like It

6 Sex, Long May It Rave

7 My Country, Sane or Otherwise

8 The War and All That

1

Mr. Nixon

Ah, the problems we face today! When I think of the problems we face today, I think first of Mr. Nixon. The problem of Mr. Nixon is so monumental and seemingly insoluble that all others dwindle to insignificance. Lord knows how many political analysts have now written books probing the problem. "What is Mr. Nixon?" they ask. Then they devote five hundred pages to concluding that Mr. Nixon is such a complex and unique problem as to surpass all human understanding. But the key to the problem is not what Mr. Nixon is; it's what Mr. Nixon isn't. What Mr. Nixon isn't, in the final analysis, is funny.

Not only is Mr. Nixon not funny, but I'm convinced he devotes every waking moment to not being funny. For twenty-five years, he has painstakingly and scrupulously avoided at all costs being funny. True, he may yet in his wisdom inaugurate an era of peace and happiness that lasts a thousand years. But I for one will never forgive him for becoming President.

Traditionally, the President is the prime target for political satire. He should be good for a column a week. There can be no question that Mr. Nixon has failed totally in fulfilling this historic duty of his high office.

Oh, for the Camelot years of Just Plain Jack, The Beautiful Society Girl he married and their faithful retainer, Portly Pierre! Oh, for the rollicking days of the rootin'-tootin' Jay Family, starring ol' Elbie Jay, the Texas wrangler who was chock full of horse sense!

But Mr. Nixon? Thanks to a quarter of a century of incredibly grueling effort he has somehow managed to become the only President in living memory who is neither too urbane, nor too earthy, too flamboyant nor too stuffy, too short nor too tall, too fat nor too thin, too athletic nor too sedentary, too . . . Mr. Nixon is simply not too anything. How do you satirize Mr. Nixon? How do you capture the comic essence of the man by exaggerating his flaws? When you find a minor one and joyfully exploit it, he immediately corrects it. He doesn't even say he wants to make one thing perfectly clear any more.

There was a time when Mr. Nixon showed promise. That was when he was a loser. He was one of the biggest losers in American political history. In rapid succession he lost the Presidency, the Governorship of California and his temper. Yet he kept coming back for more. Ah, those were the good old days!

Dick Is Back To Kick Around

Hi, there, friends in televisionland. It's time for another visit with that typical American couple, Dick and Pat, in their typical American home just around the typical American corner.

Now Dick is a typical wealthy lawyer and he'd be a typically happy and successful American except for this one terrible, personal handicap: he's got a speech problem. In fact, he can't leave the stuff alone.

As we join Dick and Pat today, Dick has just entered the door, wearing a jaunty, if somewhat guilty, expression. To cover up, he's singing gaily.

Dick (to the tune of the Battle Hymn of the Republic): I've seen the tears upon the cheeks of half a million Poles,/I've been expectorated on in sundry foreign holes . . .

Pat (*aghast*): Oh, Dear, you're singing your old campaign song! After all these years!

Dick (flustered): I was? My, I wonder what brought that to mind?

Pat (suspiciously): Where have you been?

Dick (airily): Oh, I was just having a few with the boys.

Pat: I wish you wouldn't, dear. You know how one word can lead to another. First thing you know, you'll be off on a coast-to-coast speech-making binge again and . . . Oh, dear, I can tell by your expression that you've done something awful!

Dick (confessing all): I threw my hat in the ring.

Pat (wringing her hands): But you promised. Don't you remember after that awful bash in '62? You swore off forever and told those reporters, "You'll never have me to kick around any more."

Dick: I think they've missed me. But don't worry this time, dear. I'm a new man.

Pat: You said that in '60.

Dick: I mean to say that I'm a new, new man.

Pat: You said that in '62.

Dick: Well, think of me as new, new, new man. Look, I've got a new, new, new dog and I'm going to get you a nice new, new, new cloth coat.

Pat (hopefully): Have you really changed, dear?

Dick: Changed? Just you wait till you see me in my new, new, new Homburg. (he puts it on) There. How do you like my new, new, new image of statesmanship and wide experience abroad?

Pat: It's very nice, dear, but I wouldn't talk about your experiences abroad.

Dick: And just wait till you see my new, new, new expression connoting wisdom, moderation and fair play. (he puts it on) There. Have I ever changed? Why, my own daughters wouldn't recognize me.

Trish and Julie (entering): Hi, Daddy.

Dick: How did you know it was me?

Trish: By your old, old, old five o'clock shadow.

Dick (optimistically): They say it won't show on color tee-vee.

Pat (pleadingly): Oh, please, dear, renounce temptation forever and stay at home in the bosom of your loving family.

Dick (nobly): I cannot, my love. I must go out and campaign once again, for there is a Higher Law, which no man can deny, that says this time I should win.

Pat: What law is that, dear?

Dick (confidently): The law of averages.

Well, tune in again, friends. And meanwhile, don't forget this public service message brought to you by Politicians Anonymous.

"Support your local politician—just as you would the victims of any other incurable disease."

So Mr. Nixon once again threw his hat in the ring. Once again, he was off on the old comeback trail. The concept of Mr. Nixon hitting the old comeback trail evolved into a character I came to know and love.

Kid Nixon's Secret Punch

Good morning, insomniacs. The Awful Late Show presents another chapter of that awful old movie, "The Comeback Kid," starring Kid Nixon as the aging middleweight who hasn't won a fight in 16 years and Pat as his loyal wife who wants him to quit the ring forever.

As awful old movie fans will remember, The Kid narrowly lost a championship battle on points and then hung up his gloves after a shuffling old California club fighter knocked him out two years later.

But now he's seeking another shot at the title. And he's just won an important prelim in New Hampshire by a nearly unanimous decision.

"Nobody laid a glove on me, baby," he tells Pat proudly.

"But, Kid," says Pat, "there was no one in the ring with you."

We pick up the story at that point.

The Kid (bobbing and weaving): They're afraid of me, that's why. Rocky, Ronnie Babe, all of 'em. They won't fight me in Wisconsin. They're ducking me in Nebraska. But I'm going to corner 'em in Oregon. I'll take 'em on two at a time. A left to the brisket, Rocky. A right to the choppers, Ronnie Babe. A right, a left . . .

Pat: Look out for that lamp, Kid! Oh, my, that's five you've smashed this week.

The Kid: It's lucky I wasn't using my Secret Punch. My Secret Punch would've torn the roof off. That's why they're all afraid of me, Baby. It's my Secret Punch.

Pat: Oh, Kid, do you really have a Secret Punch?

The Kid (indignantly): Did you ever hear of a challenger who didn't? But mine's a real humdinger, Baby. Wait'll they give me that shot at the title. With one Secret Punch, I'm not only going to knock out the Champ, I'm going to end the war in Vietnam.

Pat: End the war?

The Kid: That's right, Baby. I've been telling 'em everywhere, "Wait'll I'm Champ, boys, and unveil my Secret Punch on those Commie evildoers. Powie! There goes the old war!" Oh, you ought to hear 'em cheer, Baby. The Secret Punch is a real crowd pleaser.

Pat: But, Kid, if your Secret Punch will end the war, don't you think you should teach it to the Champ? Then he could end the war right now.

The Kid (frowning): I would, Baby, because I always put my country first. But my Secret Punch isn't a gimmick. It's a noble concept. A biting, gouging, headbutter could never use it—only an experienced, sporting, classy boxer like me.

Pat: Remember, Kid, I've seen you fight.

The Kid: Okay, okay. The truth is my Secret Punch is such a powerful weapon, I can't let it fall into the wrong hands. Why, if the Champ had it, there's no telling what terrible things he'd do with it.

Pat: Like what?

The Kid: Like knock out me.

Pat: I don't really believe there's such a thing as a Secret Punch.

The Kid (smiling): Don't kid yourself, Baby. Just by talking about my Secret Punch I've scared my opponents and pleased the crowd. You can't ask for more than that from a Secret Punch.

Pat: You mean that's all a Secret Punch ever does?

The Kid (happily taking her in his arms): At last, Baby, you're beginning to understand the old fight game.

The Comeback Kid Comes Back for More

Good morning, insomniacs. It's time for the Awful Late Show, featuring that awful old movie, "The Comeback Kid"—starring Dick as the middle-aged Kid, who hasn't won a fight in 16 years, and Pat as his loyal wife.

As we join them today, The Kid has climaxed his long struggle up the old comeback trail, surmounting defeats, adversity and Five O'Clock Shadow. At long last, he has won the title! By a split decision.

That's him, jubilant in victory—a Band-Aid on his jaw, one eye slightly swollen.

The Kid (happily): He never laid a glove on me. (solemnly) But I want to take this opportunity to say what a great and courageous opponent he was. One of the greatest. He never quit fighting. And I admire a fighter who never quits.

Pat: But you've been saying for months, dear, that he was nothing but a no-good bum.

The Kid: That was before I licked him.

Pat: Well, dear, I'm awfully proud of you. And now that you've achieved your goal against overwhelming odds, will you keep that promise you made in 1962 and renounce the sordid fight game forever?

The Kid (aghast): What, quit now? I'm the Champ! Don't you realize what that means? Fame! Fortune! At last you can throw away that old cloth coat. We'll be living on easy street.

Pat (dubiously): You mean all our troubles are over?

The Kid (taking her in his arms): They wrote me off as a has-been. But I got off the floor and did the impossible. And now, baby, you and I are going to enjoy the sweet fruits of victory—the adulation of the crowds, the love of the country, the . . .

Pat (happily): And no more fights, Kid?

The Kid: Not for four years. It's going to be just you and me, baby, all alone at last and . . . (The phone rings. Pat answers it.)

Pat: It's one of your handlers, Kid.

The Kid: Probably just wants to congratulate me. Hello? What do you mean the press is already speculating who'll be my sparring mate in 1972? You can tell them I'll be loyal to good old Spiro T. Whatshisname forever. Well, four years seems like forever. Yeah, I know only a minority of the fight fans are with me, but I'll win 'em over. I'll be a real crowdpleaser, you'll see. A slugfest on Capitol Hill? Sure, I know our boys are outnumbered. But we'll give 'em a battle. Yeah, I know there's a war on. Just make it clear it isn't my war. We'll fix it somehow. Riots in the ghettoes? Pollution in the streams? What about the press? Are we getting a good press? Nasty cartoons already, eh? Spiteful columnists, huh? Okay, okay, I'll be right there.

Pat (as he hangs up): Where are you going, Kid? You promised you wouldn't fight for four years.

The Kid (bobbing and weaving as he goes out the door): I know, baby, but I got to keep in training. A right to the public sector, a left to the impacted areas, a jab to Brezhnev's brisket, a right cross to the new left . . .

Pat (disconsolately after he's gone): The only thing I don't understand is why he's so happy they have him to kick around again.

The Liberals have long said you couldn't trust Mr. Nixon. By November of 1968, I was beginning to agree. Here I had finally come up with a caricature of Mr. Nixon—the lovable, punchdrunk, cauliflower-eared, perennial loser—and he thoroughly double-crossed me: he won.

Well, back to the old drawing board. Now I had followed Mr. Nixon through three campaigns. In the few private moments I had with him, I found him likable—in-

telligent, perceptive and oddly honest. But in public? Every time Mr. Nixon stepped up on a public platform, he immediately donned a mantle of frowning sincerity, a cloak of overwhelming squareness that embraced every American virtue. It was not a quality that endeared him to the somewhat cynical newsmen who covered his progress.

In the 1960 campaign, for example, both he and his opponent, John F. Kennedy, were delivering ten to twelve speeches a day—or, to be more accurate, both were delivering the same speech ten to twelve times a day. Mr. Nixon's included a number of little homilies. One that particularly jangled the nerves of newsmen concerned Mr. Nixon's dear mother and the pies she baked and sold for twenty-five cents each when he was a lad. The story was designed, presumably, to show Mr. Nixon's commanding grasp of economics. Unfortunately, it quickly palled on the newsmen and they would sit there at the press tables in the front row and chant it along with him, word for word. "My mother," Mr. Nixon and the press would begin, all wearing sincere frowns, "used to get up at five o'clock in the morning to bake her pies." Here, Mr. Nixon and the newsmen would toss their heads in unison, each flashing a little smile of shared intimacy. "Apple was my favorite . . ."

It's little wonder that the mutual antipathy between Mr. Nixon and the press has endured, to some extent, to this day. But his style went over well with his audiences and he maintained it, with a few modifications, through his 1962 and 1968 campaigns. Thus, when it came to choosing a Nixon characteristic to caricature, sincere squareness seemed a natural.

Nick Dixon Perseveres

"Great balls o' horsefeathers, Nick," Nick Dixon's new friend, Spiro Jolly, said in his comical fashion, "this sure is a nifty new clubhouse we got."

Spiro's chubby features were suffused with exuberance as the two chums explored the old white house Nick planned to take over and remodel for his Togetherness Club. There was even a hint of excitement in Nick's own sincere grey eyes.

"Yes, it certainly is, Spiro," said Nick sincerely. "I was certainly fortunate to be elected President of the Togetherness Club. It certainly proves that any poor lad can aspire to greatness, if only he has grit, perseverance, a keen mind, manly good looks, unflagging zeal and a saving humility."

At these well-spoken words, a worshipful look came over Spiro's jolly round countenance and he removed his beanie to hold it over his heart. "Golly whillikers, Nick," Spiro said admiringly, "I'm sure glad you picked me to be your A-number-one assistant. Is this my office, right here on the old ground floor?"

"No, Spiro, this is my office," Nick said sincerely. "But I certainly want you near me at all times and you will certainly be happy to know that your office is certainly no more than ten feet removed."

"Gosh all hemlock, Nick, what a spiffy honor!" said Spiro proudly. "Right or left?"

"Straight down, Spiro," said Nick sincerely. "I knew how much you wanted to serve under me. Therefore I have quartered you in the basement."

"Jehoshaphat's whiskers, Nick," said Spiro joyfully, "that's a keen idea. I'll have no way to go but up. But what'll I do, Nick?"

"Remember, Spiro, that we are all going to be members of one big team," said Nick sincerely. "We will face many challenges which we must surmount to achieve our goal of Togetherness. We must all pull together if we are to triumph."

"Golly, Nick," said Spiro eagerly, "what's our first challenge?"

"To lick the Commies," said Nick sincerely. "Then we must vanquish the militant radicals, humble the French, contain the Cubans, outwit the Russians, surround the Chinese, jail the criminals . . ."

"Great balls of molasses, Nick," interrupted Spiro jubilantly, "that's a great program for Togetherness. What other challenges does our team face?"

"We must at the same time," said Nick sincerely, "eliminate poverty, purify the streams, cleanse the air, wipe out disease, beautify the cities and, four years hence, defeat the D—crats."

"Criminy nettles, Nick," said Spiro dubiously, "I hope we haven't bitten off more'n we can chew."

"All it will take, Spiro," said Nick sincerely, "is grit, perseverance, a keen mind, manly good looks, unflagging zeal and a saving humility."

"Then, by gollies, you'll have it done in a jiffy, Nick," said Spiro elatedly. "It sure's great being a member of your winning team. What equipment should I get for me?"

"A dipper, Spiro," said Nick sincerely, placing a hand on his chum's shoulder, "and a water bucket."

Nick Dixon's Togetherness Plan

"Leaping leopards, Nick," said Nick Dixon's good friend, Spiro Jolly, in his comical fashion. "You sure picked a swell bunch of fellows to help you run your Togetherness Club."

"You certainly hit the nail on the head there, Spiro," said Nick sincerely as he looked around the table at the dozen neat, clean-cut, serious friends he had selected as his secretaries for this and that. "You are all going to make a great team for spreading Togetherness. For one thing, you all think alike."

"Excuse me, Nick . . ."

"Go right ahead, Winton," said Nick sincerely.

"I'm Maurice, Nick. He's Winton."

"And you even all look alike," said Nick sincerely.

"That's what I wanted to bring up, Nick," said Maurice eagerly. "If we are going to spread Togetherness, don't you think we should have a Negro in our gang?"

"I am glad you asked that question," said Nick sincerely. "I want the whole world to know that I gamely sought a Negro—any Negro—for a high position in our club. I personally beseeched all my friends who have the good fortune to be Negroes, but both of them refused."

"Golly Whillikers, Nick," said Spiro admiringly, "no one could do more."

"I did more, Spiro," said Nick sincerely. "I also contacted many, many Negroes whom I did not have the pleasure of knowing personally. And they, too, declined. But I am proud to say they called me by that name which is dearest to the hearts of us all, although I must modestly confess I am not one."

"Great balls o' molasses, Nick," said Spiro happily. "What name is that?"

"Mother," said Nick sincerely. "And though I sensed an undercurrent of resentment . . ."

"Criminy eye, Nick, but you're sure sharp," said Spiro approvingly.

". . . I cannot understand why," continued Nick sincerely. "I have always supported the aspirations of the Negro people and have gone out of my way to treat them as equals. Moreover, I stand ready to go on discussing their problems reasonably with any respectable Negro leader, even if it takes another 400 years."

"Jumping Jericho, Nick," said Spiro exuberantly, "They sure couldn't ask more than that."

"Therefore, my friends," said Nick sincerely, "I trust you will join in my hope that our Negro friends will see the light, enroll in our club and perform the tasks that so need doing."

"You bet your bottom dollar, Nick," said Spiro loyally. "And that reminds me, I've got to stop on the way home and get a shoeshine."

"But what if no Negroes ever join our club, Nick?" asked Maurice worriedly.

"Never fear," said Nick sincerely. "With grit, perseverance, honesty, integrity, unflagging zeal and a saving modesty, we shall win through to bring our Negro friends that which they most desire."

"What's that, Nick?"

"The spirit of Togetherness," said Nick sincerely, "whether they like it or not."

Spiro Gets His Chance

"Leaping balls of horsefeathers, Nick," said Nick Dixon's chum, Spiro T. Jolly, in his comical fashion, "tomorrow's your big day."

Nick clapped a hand on his friend's shoulder and smiled. "It's your big day, too, Spiro," he said sincerely. "We will be up there on the platform together to begin our task of spreading togetherness throughout the land."

"Gosh all hemlock, Nick," said Spiro excitedly, "you mean I'll stand right there at your side as an equal?"

"I wouldn't have it any other way, Spiro," said Nick sincerely, "that being what tradition demands. We will both take the oaths and we will both make acceptance speeches. Have you memorized the one I gave you yet?"

"Word for word, Nick," said Spiro proudly. "Want to hear me run through it? Listen." He closed his eyes tightly in concentration. "I," he recited, "do."

"That's swell, Spiro," said Nick sincerely. "Short, to the point and delivered with sincerity."

"Leaping lettuce leaves, thanks, Nick," said Spiro gratefully. A frown creased his usually jolly features. "But I sure would like to add a few words concerning the way I feel about the importance of togetherness."

"What did you have in mind, Spiro?" asked Nick sincerely.

"Criminy nettles, Nick, you know. Something like this." Spiro struck an orator's pose and said solemnly: "The chink in our armor is our failure to call a spade a spade and do our utmost to bring together all the Hunkies, Japs, Wops, Spicks, Limeys, Greasers . . ."

"I want to be perfectly candid about this, Spiro," said Nick sincerely. "No."

"Golly whiskers, Nick, I just want to help. I know, after I say, 'I do,' " asked Spiro hopefully, "could I say, 'Thank you'?"

Nick patted his friend's shoulder. "I'm afraid the program is a little long now, Spiro," he said sincerely. "You can best help in the way you've helped me so much in these past weeks—by keeping quiet. Now get some rest and I will return to take you to the ceremonies at 11 a.m."

"Golly Christmas, Nick. Will I really stand at your side?"

"I won't let you out of my sight for a minute, Spiro," Nick promised sincerely.

"And can I go to the Ball afterward?"

Nick frowned. "Well, Spiro, I want you in early," he said sincerely. "You have a long four-year stretch ahead."

"But, jumping Jeremiah, Nick, I haven't said a single thing wrong in three whole weeks," said Spiro, pouting a little. "And while I appreciate getting an outing, I think you might show a little more trust in me in my position."

Nick Dixon put an arm around his chum. "But it is precisely because of your position that you have my complete faith and trust, Spiro," he said sincerely. "Now would you like me to loosen your leg irons before I put your gag back in?"

So we came to Inauguration Day—Mr. Nixon happily looking forward to four years of challenge and power, I happily looking forward to four years of Nick Dixon & His Electric Personality. Then, on Inauguration Day, he double-crossed me again.

I remember standing there in that cold Washington air listening to his Inaugural Address—his simple, moving statements about "lowering our voices" and "bringing us together." Gone was the frowning sincerity, the mawkishness, the phoney facade of humble virtue. Gone, in a twinkling, was Nick Dixon & His Electric Personality. In his place stood a man of quiet dignity. When it was over, the newsman next to me, an old Nixon hater, turned and said with surprise, "Maybe there's hope." And maybe there was. I had always thought, and still do, that Mr. Nixon's basic problem over the years was his, forgive the word, insecurity. He was the boy from the Whittier grocery store struggling for success in a world he never made. He always seemed ill at ease. His suits—he never wore anything else—didn't fit quite right; his sense of humor was non-existent; he had no capacity whatsoever for small talk. He was the boy you let play only if it was his ball. But now he was President. Now he had reached the very top. Now he had shown them all. Moreover, the Presidency is infused with an aura of power and prestige that can't help but transmogrify mere mortals. Unquestionably, it transmogrified Mr. Nixon. The change in his demeanor was radical.

This may have been a Godsend to a troubled Nation, but what about us satirists? As the months passed during his first year in office, I became plagued by paranoid delusions that his main concern was not the affairs of State, but us. "I've done it, Pat!" he was undoubtedly crowing in the privacy of the White House. "I've become the first President in American history to thwart the political satirists. Thanks to my painstaking program of having no outstanding characteristics whatsoever, they haven't been able to lay a glove on me. At last, I've got them licked!"

But never underestimate the desperation of American satirists. Traditionally, it is our role to attack the President's weaknesses. What do you do when a President has no weaknesses? Well, you attack his strength.

A New Hero—MEDIOCREMAN!

Hi there, boys and girls. Hold on to your hats 'cause here we go—off on a thrilling new adventure series with a thrilling new hero . . . MEDIOCREMAN!

(Theme: "God Bless America.")

Faster than a committee, stronger than a peace feeler, able to leap over tall issues in a single compromise, it's . . . MEDIOCREMAN!

As we join Mediocreman today, he's in his oval office disguised as usual as the square old President of the United States, wearing his square old blue suit and talking in square old homilies. That's his pretty secretary, Lotus Lane, (who doesn't know who he really is) bustling in excitedly.

Lotus: Good gosh, Mr. President, there's a bunch of angry Congressmen and nervous aerospace industrialists out there. The Congressmen will scalp you if you don't withdraw your approval of the supersonic transport plane. And the industrialists will scalp you if you do. Oh, I sure wish Mediocreman was here.

The President: Well, Lotus, I'll admit he's been a big help. His plan to end the Vietnam war by pulling out 60,000 men a year will end it in only nine years.

Lotus: Yes, and don't forget his other ideas. Like winning approval for the ABM system by making it smaller and costlier. And placating defense critics by cutting a trifle off the Pentagon budget. And soothing college students by lowering draft calls for three months.

The President: He's saved our bacon time and again, all right. But I guess I'll have to go it alone on this SST thing and stick by my guns. Send them in, Lotus.

Lotus (shaking her head): Oh, Mr. President, you're just like all politicians—courageous but naive.

The President (after she's gone): By golly, Lotus is right. This sounds like a job for . . . MEDIOCREMAN!

(*He steps into the phone booth next to his desk and whips off his square old blue suit to reveal underneath a square old gray suit—the uniform of MEDIOCREMAN! The Congressmen and industrialists, who are stomping in, stop as though stunned.*)

Congressman: By George, it's . . . it's . . . MEDIOCRE-MAN!

Industrialist: Thank heaven you're here, Mediocreman. These short-sighted penny-pinchers want to kill that $600 million for our SST. America will lose its world leadership in commercial aviation. Everybody else has an SST.

Congressman: You call a plane that'll leave a 50-mile swath of shattered windows, crockery and nerves in its wake leadership?

Industrialist (angrily): Listen, you old fogey . . .

Congressman (doubling his fist): Who's an old fogey?

Mediocreman (fixing each with his 32-tooth smile): My 20-20 vision sees the only possible solution. You Congressmen must appropriate $300 million for half an SST—thus saving the taxpayers $300 million.

Industrialist: But Mediocreman, half an SST will fly only half as fast.

Mediocreman: Exactly! America will continue its leadership by having an SST. But it will create no sonic booms to destroy property.

(*The Congressmen and Industrialists embrace and depart. Mediocreman dons his square old blue suit before Lotus Lane enters again.*)

Lotus: Good gosh, Mr. President, they sure left happy. They said Mediocreman solved the whole thing. Why can't you be more like him?

The President: Well Lotus, we can't all be mediocre. (Winking at the camera.) But I promise you, I'll keep on trying.

Mediocreman Meets the Press

Hold on to your hats, boys and girls, 'cause here we go—off on another thrilling adventure with that hero of our times—MEDIOCREMAN!

Faster than a Government study group, stronger than a joint resolution, able to straddle tall fences in a single straddle, it's . . . MEDIOCREMAN!

As we join Mediocreman today, kids, he's seated behind his square desk in the Oval Room, disguised as a stuffy old President. Just entering is his secretary, Lotus Lane (who doesn't suspect his real identity). She looks worried.

Lotus: Gosh sakes, Mr. President, the press is outside and they're loaded for bear. They're going to ask you straight out just what your plans are for the problems the country faces. What are you going to do?

The President: Send them in, Miss Lane, I shall give them honest, straightforward answers.

Lotus (skittering out): Holy cow, then are we in trouble! Oh, I wish Mediocreman were here.

The President (to himself): Lotus is right. This sounds like a job for . . . MEDIOCREMAN!

(*He whips off his stuffy old blue suit to reveal underneath a stuffy old gray suit—the uniform of . . . MEDIOCREMAN!*)

First Reporter (entering): Mr. Pres . . . Oh, it's Mediocreman! Thank heavens you're here. Tell us, sir, what do you plan to do about integration?

Mediocreman: Well, to be perfectly candid, I plan to steer a middle course between those demanding instant integration and those seeking to maintain segregation forever.

Second Reporter: And how long, sir, will it take to achieve the school desegregation ordered by the Supreme Court 15 years ago?

Mediocreman: Only as long—and let me be perfectly clear about this—as absolutely necessary.

Third Reporter: What about tax reform, sir? The public is up in arms over these millionaires who pay no taxes whatsoever.

Mediocreman: We shall double their tax bills next year! I seek the middle ground between the rich who pay no taxes and the poor who do. As for tax evaders, we are giving them 15 years to comply with the law and no extensions will be granted—unless absolutely necessary.

Fourth Reporter: On pollution, sir . . .

Mediocreman: I plan to steer a middle course between those who want clean air and water and those who want pollution. By 1984, Americans will be able to take a dip in any river or lake—up to their waists.

Fifth Reporter: About Vietnam, sir . . .

Mediocreman: I shall continue to seek the middle ground between those who want instant withdrawal and those who would fight there forever. By withdrawing half our forces and limiting combat to Mondays, Wednesdays and Fridays, I shall force the enemy to surrender in 15 years—unless more time is absolutely necessary.

Sixth Reporter: About the nomination of Judge Haynsworth, sir . . .

Mediocreman: Let me be very candid about this. I am attempting to steer a middle course between those who want an honest Supreme Court Justice and those who want a dishonest one.

The Reporters (rushing out): Thank you, Mediocreman.

Lotus Lane (entering after Mediocreman has resumed his disguise): Oh, Mr. President, I saw it all on television! Wasn't Mediocreman wonderful?

The President (smiling): He certainly was, Miss Lane. (staring sincerely into the camera) As Mediocreman always says, "There's a right answer and a wrong answer to all our problems—and the solution lies somewhere in between."

Mediocreman Vs. Santa Claus

Faster than a Senate confirmation, more powerful than an inflationary curb, able to straddle tall issues in a single straddle, it's . . . MEDIOCREMAN!

As we join Mediocreman today, kids, he's in his stuffy Oval Office disguised as the mild-mannered President. His pretty secretary, Lotus Lane (who doesn't know his true identity) enters, looking worried.

Lotus: Terrible news, Mr. President. Inflation's running away. And with holiday shoppers on the loose, prices will go out of sight. Christmas this year will ruin the country!

The President: Well, Lotus, perhaps if I issued a strongly-worded attack against Christmas . . .

Lotus (Angrily): You'd be crucified! What good would that do? (stomping out) Oh, I wish Mediocreman were here.

The President: Hmmm, I think Lotus is right. This sounds like a job for Mediocreman!

(*He quickly whips off his stuffy old blue suit to reveal underneath a stuffy old gray suit, the uniform of . . . MEDIOCREMAN! He pushes a secret button under his desk and up through a trap door pops his trusty sidekick . . . Spiro-Hero!*)

Spiro-Hero (saluting): You called, Chief?

Mediocreman: Right Spiro. I wanted to tell you what good jobs you've been doing for me lately.

Spiro-Hero (glowing): You mean my statesmanlike appraisal of those effete, intellectual, impudent, snobbish, ideological eunuchs who are parasites of passion?

Mediocreman: I couldn't have put it better myself, Spiro, if I weren't trying to lower my voice and bring the people

together.

Spiro-Hero (modestly): I consider it my sacred duty, Chief, to stand up before the people, come what may, and speak your mind.

Mediocreman: And let me say how much I admired your courage in taking on the television networks, the most powerful opinion-molding force in history.

Spiro-Hero (stoutly): I sure showed that tiny, closed fraternity of privileged men that their querulous criticism can't scare us—without involving you in any way, sir.

Mediocreman: Right, Spiro. And now I've got another job for you—Christmas.

Spiro-Hero (beaming): Oh, good, Chief. I'm all for Christmas.

Mediocreman (frowning): I'm against it.

Spiro-Hero (still beaming): I'm against it. Oh, I'll rip cheap, tawdry, maudlin Christmas up one side and down the other. I'll tell the kids there's no Santa Claus and I'll . . .

Mediocreman (clapping him on the back): That's the ticket, Spiro. And when they attack and revile and castigate you, take heart in the knowledge that you are keeping my sacred promise—namely that they won't have me to kick around any more.

(*Later, Lotus and the President are watching Spiro-Hero on television as he wallops "the effete merchants of snobbish inflation who fatten their coffers on the parasites of the Christmas passion."*)

Lotus (admiringly): I hear Mediocreman put him up to it to save the country. (angrily) Oh, why can't you be more like Mediocreman?

The President (winking into the camera after she's stormed out): Never forget, kids, that when the time comes for a man to stand up and take a dangerous position, a good leader will always find one to stand up and take it.

But as time passed, I grew uneasy with the character of Mediocreman. It wasn't the outrage of the Conservatives that bothered me, it was the praise from the Liber-

als. "You're really showing up that Tricky Dick," they would say, bubbling with vitriol. But if there's one thing that warns you've erred in your analysis of Mr. Nixon, it's the Liberals agreeing with you. For twenty-five years they've hated Mr. Nixon for what he was twenty-five years ago. The more I thought about it, the more I felt I was being unfair. To be fair, whatever else Mr. Nixon wasn't, he wasn't mediocre. He was an intelligent, driving, ambitious man—certainly no mediocrity. Moreover, he was now trying to bring the country together and at the same time erase his twenty-five-year-old reputation as a politician with an instinct for the jugular. This he was doing by scrupulously avoiding saying anything unkind about anyone. Fair is fair. So I attacked him for that.

Dick Nixon, Sportscaster

"There's nothing I'd like better than to have Bud's (football broadcaster Bud Wilkinson's) job."

—President Richard M. Nixon at the Texas-Arkansas football game in Fayetteville, Ark.

Hi. Hi, there, folks. Well, here we are in the closing minutes of what, in my judgment, is certainly the game of the century. To be very candid, I don't think I've seen a more exciting game of the century, in my opinion, since last week's game of the century in Pocatello, Idaho.

Now I want to make one thing perfectly clear. In the past I have indicated that the winner of this gallant struggle between Texas and Arkansas today will be the number one team in the country. I have received some criticism on this.

And let me just say on that score that I certainly didn't intend to indicate that the loser wouldn't also be the number one team in the country. Along with Penn State. Not to mention a number of other number one teams in this great land of ours.

It would be very easy to say that the winner today will be the only number one team in the country. But a sportscaster has the heavy burden of doing what's right—right for the fans, right for players and right for all the number one teams in the country.

Well, now, I see that time is back in on the field, it seems to me. I would say that Texas has the ball—I don't want to prejudge the officials on this. I don't always agree with the officials. Many decent Americans don't. But let me point out that what the officials say is, in my opinion, the law and it is the duty of a sportscaster, in my judgment, to uphold the law, whether he agrees with it or not.

But I would say that Texas has the ball in the vicinity of, as I indicated in an earlier statement to you at that time, the Arkansas 42-yard line. I say this somewhat cautiously, as I don't want to preclude the hopes of the millions of Arkansas fans, whom I admire highly, that Arkansas may, at some point in the future, also have the ball. But at this time, that would be my observation.

Yes, Texas, I'm proud to say, does have the ball. The quarterback is fading back to—and I do not say this to limit his options in any way—pass. Yes, he has instituted a pass and, quite candidly, it is the finest pass I have ever seen. A perfect spiral, it seems to me.

By this, I do not mean to detract in any manner from the Arkansas quarterback, who has also thrown many of the finest passes I have ever, in my judgment, seen. All perfect spirals, it seems to me.

Well, there's the final gun, my fellow Americans. The two number one teams in the country are now staging a planned withdrawal from the field, just as I confidently predicted they would at this time.

Let me be perfectly honest on one thing: I don't think this is the time or the place, in my judgment, to make any emotional statement on who won or lost this game of the century today.

In my opinion, this would amount to kicking the loser when he's down. I have never kicked losers when they are down and I do not intend to start in now. That is my position on this matter, rightly or wrongly.

But I would say, in my opinion, that it's been a pleasure, in my judgment, bringing you this sportscast today. It seems to me.

And yet how far can you go with your President as a football broadcaster? For one thing, football season lasts only ten months a year these days. For another, Mr.

Nixon didn't seem to be doing too well in bringing us together. In fact, I was rapidly developing the theory that he'd do better to keep us apart.

There was still one minor facet of Mr. Nixon's personality that I hadn't yet tried to exploit: his simplistic method of explaining complex subjects. When he goes on television, there's always a bit of the second-grade schoolteacher in him.

Dick and Pat See the Bums

Look, Dick, look and see. See those people outside our nice white house. They do not look like tourists. Are they tourists, Dick?

No, Pat, no. They are not tourists. They are bums. They are bums because they believe in violence. Violence is bad. I deplore violence. Violence never solves anything. Violence gets people killed. Violence is very bad.

I see, Dick. They are bums because they do violent things. What violent things do they do, Dick?

They throw rocks, Pat. They burn buildings. They march across boundary lines without permits. They cause police to club and shoot them.

Oh, Dick, those are bad things. Why do the bums do these bad things?

They are angry, Pat. They are angry at the war. They want me to stop the war. They do these bad things to make me stop the war.

They are silly, Dick. They are silly to do bad things to make you stop the war. You cannot stop a war by doing bad things.

You are right, Pat. Violence only begets violence. But the bums are even more angry now. They are more angry because they think I have made a bigger war. They are more angry because I marched our soldiers across the boundary line into Cambodia.

Did you have a permit, Dick?

I do not need a permit, Pat. I can march our soldiers anywhere I want, if I think it is right.

Why do the bums think you have made a bigger war, Dick?

They do not understand, Pat. I did not march into Cambodia to make a bigger war. I marched into Cambodia to make a smaller war.

I understand, Dick. Is it going well?

Yes, Pat. We have burned many buildings. We have killed many people. It is going very well.

Oh, Dick, these sound like bad things.

Let me be candid, Pat. I deplore burning buildings. I deplore killing people. But we must do these things in order to stop the war.

How will doing these things stop the war, Dick?

By doing these things, Pat, we will make Hanoi stop the war just because we politely ask it to.

Oh, Dick, you are so brave and good. You are so brave and good to do these things to make Hanoi stop the war.

Yes, Pat. I do not like to do these things. But I must make Hanoi listen to us. I must make Hanoi stop the war.

Oh, Dick, listen. Listen to those bums. They are shouting. They are yelling. They are doing bad things.

Close the window, Pat. I will not listen to a bunch of bums who do bad things.

Yes, Dick. But why do they think doing bad things will make you stop the war? Where do they get such ideas?

I do not know, Pat. But I have a wish. I wish these bums would be more like us.

But once again the device failed. Just as Mr. Nixon isn't mediocre enough to be Mediocreman, so he isn't simplistic enough for a series like Dick and Pat. It was time to face the bitter truth: whatever Mr. Nixon is, he can't be satirized. Not being able to attack him for what he is, I therefore, in a last desperate, dying effort, decided to attack him for what he isn't. What he isn't, of course, is funny.

Dick Is Only Human

"I want you to be perfectly candid about this, Pat. Do you, in your opinion, consider me dull, stuffy or, let the chips fall where they may, not human enough?"

"I have always thought of you, Dick, as human."

"Thank you, Pat, for your confidence. For more than a month now my aides have attempted to project a new image of me, emphasizing my warmly human qualities that make me, in my judgment, a regular fellow, one of the boys. Yet, for reasons that are unclear, the polls indicate our efforts have, in the final analysis, failed."

"I'm sure it's not your fault, Dick."

"Let me say this about that, Pat, As it was a question of voter appeal and thus of major importance, I decided to cooperate fully. That was my decision on this."

"Was it difficult, Dick?"

"I did not take the easy path for that is not, rightly or wrongly, my way. I appeared on the Today Show to prove I was a regular fellow. I granted countless televised interviews during which, though I sat in a straight-backed chair, I crossed my legs to show I was one of the guys. And, to illustrate that I was warmly human, I allowed the photographers to take my picture while strolling on the beach in casual attire."

"Yes, Dick, I had never seen a more informal photograph of you—wearing that windbreaker with the Presidential seal on it and only a hint of your sincere blue necktie showing."

"I even considered Ron's request that I remove my shoes for the occasion to show my disdain for formality. But, in the end, I was forced to reject the concept, not wishing to get my socks wet."

"What more can you do, Dick?"

"Well, Pat, the staff feels I should be the subject of warm, earthy anecdotes like the press told about Lyndon. But they haven't thought of any yet."

"Give them another month, Dick. Wait, what about the time you spilled catsup on your vest and said, 'Darn it!' "

"That language, in my judgment, is not necessary. But perhaps if I told a joke. Hmmmm. Aha, listen: 'I have both won and lost. Winning is more fun.' What is your candid opinion of that joke, Pat?"

"I think it is the funniest joke you ever told, Dick."

"Thank you, Pat, for your confidence. I shall now, having slept my 7 hours and 32 minutes as always, leap from this bed and devote my usual 4 minutes and 47 seconds to my breakfast so that I may stride to work. Please order my regular bowl of cottage cheese and catsup."

"Wait, Dick, I have a good idea. Why not have breakfast in bed this morning?"

"What is breakfast in bed, Pat?"

"Many people have breakfast in bed, Dick. I'll call in the photographers. It will give you a warmly human image that will capture the hearts of all Americans."

"By golly, Pat, you are right. Wait 'til I adjust this pillow behind me. There, now how can anyone say I am not a regular fellow, just one of the guys. How do I look?"

"Fine, Dick, But maybe if you just loosened your necktie. . . ."

That column, I think, came closer to capturing Mr. Nixon than any of the others. But it doesn't make a series. If you keep telling your readers that your central character isn't the slightest bit funny, they may come to believe you and turn to the comic page. Thus, after years of striving, I threw in the towel. I still write about Mr. Nixon. I grouch about his political ploys or his image-making techniques. But in these columns he is merely President Nixon, an undifferentiated human being. Dull as dish-

water.

Nor have I alone failed. Cartoonists have concentrated on his ski-jump nose; mimics have captured his speech mannerisms. But these merely reflect the surface. No satirist has yet discovered his comic essence. And, to me, this is the prime clue to the nature of the man.

Mr. Nixon is the first President in political memory who can't be caricatured. Roosevelt, Truman, Eisenhower, Kennedy and Johnson were easy. Each had a human quality you could lovingly exploit—flamboyance, temper, fatherliness, elan or folksiness. Some, like Mr. Kennedy, wanted to be admired. Some, like Mr. Johnson, wanted to be loved. But Mr. Nixon, it seems to me, wants, above all, to be respected. For twenty-five years the press has kicked him around. Now he's on top. He wants, above all, the respect he feels he has rightfully earned. The last thing this basically-insecure man who grew up in a Whittier grocery store and fought his way through the tangled thickets of politics to fame and fortune wants is to be laughed at.

If so, he's succeeded admirably. Ask yourself when you last heard a Nixon joke—the kind that made the rounds about each of his predecessors. Never in recent times, my fellow Americans, have we had a President who was less of a laughing stock.

So to the polls, ye sons of freedom! Think of the grimness settling slowly over the land. Think of the dying heritage of American political humor. Think of me. And kindly cast your vote for George Wallace.

Thank you.

PART TWO

MY OTHER PROBLEMS

(Which are relatively insignificant)

2

The Environment

And Other Disaster Areas

The Day the Landlord Quit

Scene: The Heavenly Real Estate Office. The Landlord, looking a bit tired, is seated on his Heavenly Throne. His business agent, Mr. Gabriel, is standing by, trumpet in hand.

The Landlord (wearily): There. Now that I have all the galaxies wheeling in their proper courses, is there anything else demanding immediate attention?

Mr. Gabriel: Well, Sir, I've been meaning to tell You about Earth. That's a tiny planet revolving around a third-rate sun on the fringes of . . .

The Landlord (testily): How can I forget it? It's more trouble than all the rest. I suppose the tenants are still running down the property?

Mr. Gabriel (consulting his record book): Yes, Sir. More gouges bulldozed in the mountain meadows. More holes napalmed in the forested carpets. More species of livestock exterminated on the fruited plains. More . . .

The Landlord (angrily): By Me, who do they think they are? Vengeance is mine, saith I. And I think it's high time I wreaked a little.

Mr. Gabriel (raising his trumpet): Yes, Sir. But I think you ought to know, before I blow the eviction notice, that . . .

The Landlord: No need for such a drastic measure, Gabriel. I shall easily teach them the error of their ways by some single awful visitation of my wrath. I know! (He shudders.) I shall pollute the waters from which they drink and the very air they breathe.

Mr. Gabriel: I'm afraid, Sir, that they're very busy doing just that themselves.

The Landlord (frowning): Then I shall invent a new disease with which to plague them.

Mr. Gabriel: Frankly, Sir, there's nothing they've become more adept at than inventing new diseases. Hardly a day goes by that . . .

The Landlord (thoughtfully): I suppose I could visit the sins of the fathers upon the children.

Mr. Gabriel: A well-established practice down there, Sir. They call it "race relations."

The Landlord: Hmmm. Do you think wars and rumors of wars would do any good?

Mr. Gabriel: I don't think they'd notice, Sir.

The Landlord (sternly): They go too far. Blow, Gabriel! I shall rain fire and destruction from the sky upon their cities to teach them that vengeance is mine.

Mr. Gabriel (hesitantly): Yes, Sir. But I think I should point out that they're perfectly capable of doing that themselves. Indeed, if you rain death and destruction on one of their cities, they will immediately rain it on the others, seeking vengeance on each other.

The Landlord: Good Me, Gabriel! Do you realize what you're saying?

Mr. Gabriel (reluctantly): Yes, Sir. That's what I've been meaning to tell you: there's nothing we can do to them that they haven't already done to themselves.

The Landlord (with a sigh of defeat): Well, Gabriel, at least we know who they think they are.

Now, Brethren, Let Us Spray

Man's triumph over insects, after a million-year battle, came with the para-dioxogenous-quyxylytylpytl. Or, as it was commonly called, PDQ.

PDQ represented a giant stride forward from such early crude insecticides as DDT. It was not only 16.3 times more toxic, 12.8 times longer lasting, and 6.3 times cheaper to produce, but it never gummed up the sprayer.

Moreover, exhaustive laboratory tests proved it was absolutely harmless to test tubes, beakers, rubber tubing and Bunsen burners.

As always, a few conservative, fuddy-duddy scientists cautioned that no one knew what the long-range effects of PDQ might be.

"Exactly!" cried a PDQ's discoverer, Dr. Greengrass Grommet. "And therefore no one can show that PDQ will produce any harmful, long-range effects whatsoever.

"These very same Nervous Nellies protested 237 scientific discoveries in the past on the very same grounds. And in every single case time proved them wrong. Can we let these wrong-headed fuddy-duddies stand in the way of progress?"

As always, Dr. Grommet and his progress-minded colleagues won the battle and PDQ was approved for sale with adequate warnings on the label.

Housewives gleefully sprayed flies with it. Health officers happily sprayed fleas with it. Foresters joyfully sprayed bark beetles with it. And farmers delightedly sprayed boll weevils with it.

In five short years, the world was sopping wet with PDQ.

And just as Dr. Grommet had predicted, not a fly, flea, bark beetle, boll weevil or any other insect flew, crawled or bored anywhere.

"After a million years of swatting midges, mosquitoes and miscellaneous malefactors," crowed Dr. Grommet, "mankind can at last enjoy the birds and the bees and the flowers in peace."

But, of course, there weren't any. Without insects to eat, the birds disappeared. And without bees to do their thing, the flowers pined.

Yet this was a small price to pay for an insect-free world. And no one would have minded too much if, in the seventh year, all the trees hadn't fallen down.

"Who needs trees?" said Dr. Grommet with a frown. "Never forget that, thanks to PDQ, we have doubled production on our crops." Which, in the ninth year, failed to come up.

"Never fear, we shall find new ways to harvest the fish from the sea," said Dr. Grommet desperately. And the new way was found in the tenth year when all the fish helpfully floated to the surface. Belly up.

And so it went. Finally, the last man on earth, who just happened to be Dr. Grommet, sat on a mountain top gloomily surveying the barren, lifeless planet.

"I don't want to carp, dear," said the last woman on earth, who just happened to be Mrs. Grommet, "but it looks as though all those fuddy-duddy scientists were right and you were wrong."

"Ah, but never forget that they were wrong 237 times," said Dr. Grommet proudly. "And I was only wrong once."

Affluence Is a Lot of Garbage

Looking back on it now, the straw that broke America's back was the advent of the no-deposit, no-return bottle.

For a generation, Americans had paid a two-cent deposit on their soft drink and beer bottles. No decent American, imbued with Yankee thrift, could bear to throw one away.

Instead, he would store his empty bottles on the back porch until the collection threatened to topple. Then he would wearily trundle them all back to the store, grumbling all the way.

This drudgery hurt sales. But in the 1950s the manufacturers came up with a brilliant solution: they would simply charge an extra nickel for the beverage and tell the customer to throw the two-cent bottle away.

Sales soared. A decade later Americans were happily heaving out 30 million no-deposit, no-return bottles a day. Guilt-free.

It was the beginning of the Nation's new Never-Use-Anything-Twice Syndrome.

Newspapers, which had once been saved for the Boy Scout drive, were handed to the overburdened trash man. The re-usable milk bottle was replaced by the throw-away carton. The cost of garbage removal sky-rocketed.

By 1969 an economist estimated that it cost the average city 30 cents to cart off and bury an empty soft drink bottle—or seven times what it cost to make. And the New York Times, with presumably mixed feelings, reported: "In New York City it costs more to dispose of The Sunday Times than it costs to buy it."

But an affluent society could care less. Disposable clothes

("Save on cleaning bills!") were followed by disposable table settings ("Simply bundle it all up in the disposable damask tablecloth and throw it away!")

Disposable bathtubs ("No more unsightly rings!") and disposable carpets ("End vacuuming forever!") culminated in the 1975 G.E. Disposable Kitchen ("Push a button and watch your housework go down the drain!").

It seemed as though everything Americans touched turned into garbage.

But as more and more disposable products were developed, they became less and less disposable—there being no room left to dispose of them.

A worried Government experimented with compressing garbage into building blocks, the only foreseeable solution. But the public, with its new Never-Use-Anything-Twice Syndrome complained, "Who wants to live in a pile of garbage?"

The end came with the introduction of the 1979 GT Two-plus-Six Disposable Sedan ("Save on repair bills!") When it broke down, the motorist simply got out, slammed the door (which usually fell off) and walked away.

In the choked streets, transportation, including garbage trucks, came to a standstill. As the mounds grew higher, the American culture literally vanished from the face of the earth.

Years later, anthropologists studying the mounds called them "the greatest monuments to an affluent culture the world has ever seen—higher than the Acropolis, more vast than Angkor Wat." At least, they added, "we think there's a culture down under there somewhere."

But it was an historian who, after perusing a copy of "A Disposable History of 20th Century America" found in the litter, grasped the moral of the tragedy:

"A no-deposit, no-return bottle," he said, "isn't worth two cents."

Bridging the Garbage Gap

With the American land mass in danger of vanishing beneath an ever-growing mound of garbage, scientists have been working around the clock to meet the threat head-on.

At long last, it can now be reported, a brilliant technological breakthrough offers new hope of stemming the tide of swill.

The development is the work of a research team at the West Newton Institute of Technology, headed by Dr. Russell Zimmerman. It employs a freeze-dry technique similar to that now used to condense coffee and tea.

In laboratory experiments, Dr. Zimmerman was able to reduce 1.3 metric tons of garbage to a 16-ounce jar of shimmering crystals. He calls the resultant product, logically enough, "Instant Garbage."

At first glance, the demand for Instant Garbage would appear minimal. But a two-year study by the Passaic Center for Peace & War Research foresees "unlimited possibilities in an ever-expanding world market."

As the center's report points out, "Americans today enjoy the highest per capita rate of garbage production (3285 pounds annually) of any nation on earth. Measured either by weight or by volume, the yearly U.S. production of garbage far exceeds that of automobiles, field crops and non-ferrous metals combined.

"Garbage," the report states flatly, "is by far and away the number one product of our free enterprise system. It must be shared with the less fortunate abroad.

"In country after country, we find a direct and unvarying

correlation between the standard of living and the amount of garbage available—the less garbage, the lower the standard of living. From these statistics, it is obvious that only by increasing garbage production can the underprivileged nations ever hope to reach the economic takeoff point.

"What has prevented us in the past from sending this bountiful fruit from our horn of plenty to our needy friends overseas has been the high shipping costs. Instant Garbage," concludes the report, "provides the answer."

One 16-ounce jar of Instant Garbage, when mixed with water, the report notes, would supply the average Asian or African peasant with enough top-quality American garbage to last him a year.

"Surely this is a more practical and humanitarian goal for our Foreign Aid Program," says the report, "than sending him bullets and bombs."

While the report does not go into the military uses of Instant Garbage, it is known the Pentagon has the matter under study. Dropped in the enemy's rivers and streams, Instant Garbage would create instant pollution. Scattered on the enemy's land area prior to a rainfall, the crystals might well undermine his will to resist.

"There is every possibility," says one General in R&D hopefully, "that we may be able to stem the tide of world communism with 100 percent American garbage."

Experts have warned, however, that at present the U.S. lacks the garbage capacity for both military and peaceful uses. They estimate production would have to double before America could hope to cover the entire planet in even a minimum blanket of garbage.

But most observers feel that given American know-how and the ingrained American determination to scatter garbage, this is a feasible goal to include in the American dream of making the world more like America.

Conservationists—Drop Dead

Once upon a time there was a man of good will named Goodwyn Goodwill whose only desire was to leave the world a better place for his passing through it. And he was happy.

He had a happy wife and three happy children and they lived in a happy house with a happy dog and a happy cat. And they had a lovely garden.

Then one day Goodwill took up the study of ecology—ecology having suddenly become quite the rage.

The first thing he read was that pesticides were leaching from the soil to poison the waters of the ocean. "I can't poison the waters of the ocean," he said. So he renounced pesticides and let the snails take over the garden.

The next thing he read was that the smoke and fumes he produced were befouling the crystalline air. "I can't befoul the crystalline air," he said. So he gave up smoking, driving the family car and fires in the fireplace.

Then he read that overgrazing by livestock was causing serious soil erosion. "I can't erode the soil of my planet," he said. So he gave up meat and wearing leather products—going barefoot summer and winter.

Goodwill felt he was now at least holding his own until he read that he, personally, required more than seven tons of fuel each year to warm, transport, and illuminate himself. And he was thus destroying at a prodigious rate irreplaceable reserves of coal and oil that nature had taken eons to create.

"Good heavens!" he cried dazedly. And he turned off the furnace, doused the lights and gave up riding the bus.

In his cold, dark house, he could now read only in the

daytime. This was fortunate because it was a full week before he stumbled across still another staggering statistic: He, personally, required no less than five tons of food, minerals and forest products each and every year to maintain himself in a civilized state.

Worse yet, he threw away annually, all by himself, one ton of beer cans, pop bottles, milk cartons and other empty containers that now littered a once pristine America.

To save on food, a panicky Goodwill went on a strict diet, eating nothing but dandelion greens and boiled thistles.

To save on minerals, he eschewed tinfoil, ballpoint pens and loose change.

And to preserve the forests, he swore never to read anything printed on paper again.

That was good. Because a full month passed before Goodwill heard on his neighbor's radio a scientist explaining how each of us breathes in life-giving oxygen and breathes out poisonous carbon dioxide.

It was then that the awful truth hit him: "On this overcrowded planet," he said to himself, "the only way a man can stop doing harm to the ecology is to drop dead."

So he gave up breathing.

His last wish was to take up as little space as possible in death. Thus he was cremated and his ashes scattered. Most of his remains therefore became smog. And his ashes, containing ten parts per million of indestructible DDT, washed down to the poisoned sea.

Moral: As you go through life, don't worry about doing the most possible good. Just worry about doing the least possible harm.

Babies Are a Lot of Garbage

Time: an evening in 1984. Scene: the modest living room of John and Mary. It is their third wedding anniversary. Mary is seated before the fire, knitting.

John (glancing up from his paper): What's that you're knitting, dear?

Mary (nervously): Oh, just a pair of booties.

John: That's ni . . . (alarmed) A what?

Mary (blushing): I didn't know how to tell you, dear. You see, I'm going to have a . . . (blurting it out) Well, I'm going to have a baby.

John (leaping to his feet): Good grief, Mary! How could you?

Mary: It just happened. But, really, John, we can afford a child.

John: I know that, Mary. But what are we going to tell our friends?

Mary: We'll just tell them the truth, that's all.

John: Where have you been for the past ten years? You know how everyone feels about people having babies. Oh, I've been so proud of us. When someone looked at me suspiciously and asked, "How many children do you have?" I could hold my head up and say, "None!" but now . . .

Mary: Other couples still have babies. Remember just last year the Granniches down in the next block . . .

John: And remember what everybody said about them. Selfish, careless, anti-ecological environment despoilers—that was about the kindest remark. (wistfully) You know, just last week George Peedy was passing around cigars at the office and we all clapped him on the back and shook his hand . . .

Mary: See. He was proud his wife had a baby.

John: No, she had an abortion. I don't suppose . . .

Mary: It's too late. But, John, I think it's silly. I don't see what harm one tiny, little baby's going to do . . .

John (shocked): What harm? Haven't you been following the Department of Ecology's warnings—newspapers, billboards, radio, television. This child of yours will produce 68.2 tons of garbage, 34.6 tons of air pollutants, and I forget how many tons of industrial wastes. He will consume 46.3 tons of irreplaceable resources such as coal and oil, 38.3 tons of towering redwoods, juniper and pine, 68.2 tons of . . .

Mary (disbelieving): A little baby, doing all that?

John: He will during his lifetime, Mary. This child, for which you are responsible, will unarguably help destroy our environment.

Mary: Oh, John can't you think of him as your child?

John (brightening): I was going to ask you about that, Mary. Now, you didn't by any chance have an affair with the milkman, did you? (hopefully) Or that nice-looking television repairman? Or . . .

Mary (tearfully): Oh, John, you're being horrid!

John (shrugging): I was just hoping I wasn't responsible, that's all.

Mary: How can you deny your own child? For a million years, men have been proud of becoming fathers.

John: They didn't realize what they were doing. But now that the ecologists have shown us what an awesome crime against nature it is . . .

Mary (throwing herself at his feet): Please, dearest, try to share my happiness. Just think, together we are creating God's greatest gift—a cuddly, pink, glowing, beautiful baby!

John (turning away in disdain): It may be a baby to you. But to us ecology-oriented citizens, Mary, it's just 68.2 tons of garbage.

The Automobile Explosion

The League for Planned Automobiles held another grim rally to warn the world once again of the gravest threat it faces: The Automobile Explosion.

Dr. Paul Horlick, author of "The Automobile Bomb" and other best-sellers, laid the frightening facts on the line:

In 1900, there were only 8000 automobiles on the Nation's highways. Today, there are more than 100,000,000.

"The number of automobiles has soared at almost precisely the ratio predicted by the great demographer, Malthus," said Dr. Horlick. "Thus we see that by the year 2000, under the inexorable dictates of Malthusian Law, America will be trying to support no fewer than 4.3 trillion automobiles!"

Dr. Horlick painted a bleak picture of America in the year 2000, covered from coast to coast with a solid blanket of cars, in some areas two and three deep.

The land, he said, would be swept with "terrible gasoline famines" and the carnage on the highways would be incredible.

"If 100 million cars cause 55,000 deaths a year today," he pointed out, "then 4.3 trillion cars will inevitably cause 2.3 million deaths a year."

Added to this, he said, would be the effects of overcrowding on the driver: "Imagine the psychoses caused by having to wait six weeks for an opening in the traffic pattern to get your car out of the garage."

Dr. Horlick blamed the Automobile Explosion on two factors: an ever-increasing production rate and a longer life span. "Thanks to advances in modern motor care," he said, "the life expectancy of the average car has more than doubled since 1925."

Dr. Horlick is founder of an organization known as "Zero Automobile Growth." Its goal is to induce all Americans to have no more than 1.2 cars per family.

"Through adequate family planning," he said, "we can and must prevent careless citizens from cluttering up the highways by having unwanted cars."

Research showed, he said, that most people had unwanted cars as the result of "yielding to a sudden urge without taking adequate precautions."

A typical case, he said, would be that of a man who passes a dealer's showroom, sees a Belchfire-8 in the window, and, to prove his masculinity, consummates the deal on the spot.

To prevent such accidents, Dr. Horlick made an impassioned plea for increased distribution through Planned Automobile Clinics of The Pill (a simple tranquilizer effective in suppressing such urges).

For Catholics, he recommended the Rhythm Method, whereby couples visit automobile dealers only between midnight and 4 a.m., when the showroom is closed.

As a last resort, Dr. Horlick called for an all-out educational campaign "aimed at convincing American families to have babies instead."

"Babies," he noted, "not only take up less space than automobiles, but they consume less of our irreplaceable natural resources and are, of course, smog-free.

"Moreover, while the upkeep is about the same, the initial cost of a baby is far lower. To save our vanishing heritage, we must show every American that a baby is a better deal."

Unfortunately, Dr. Horlick conceded gloomily, the statistics on growth rates prove conclusively that most Americans would rather have a car.

The Crockery Crisis

The news that the Russians were developing a Giant Crockery Smasher (GCS) caught Washington completely by surprise.

A worried President immediately called an emergency session of the National Security Council.

"It's worse than we thought at first, Mr. President," Henry Kissinger reported gravely. "The Russian GCS is 90 per cent complete. When installed in the Kremlin, its supersonic beam will create a 50-mile-wide swath of smashed crockery, broken windows and jangled nerves stretching from Moscow to the Urals."

"Worse yet, sir," said Mr. Kissinger. "Even when operating at subsonic levels, the noise from the Russian GCS will drive strong men up the walls. Moreover, its emissions into the upper atmosphere will raise temperatures 13 per cent, thereby melting the polar ice caps and sending huge tides to destroy the coastal cities of the world."

"We must stem the rising tides of Communism!" muttered the President grimly.

"Worst," said Mr. Kissinger, "the French and the British have combined to build a GCS and hope to corner the Free World market in crockery smashers."

"Let me make one thing perfectly clear, gentlemen," said the President with determination. "We must at all costs maintain America's world leadership in crockery smashing."

When the issue was put to Congress on this patriotic basis, a bill to appropriate $63.2 million for initial designs passed without a dissenting vote.

With America already several years behind the Russians,

French and British, there was obviously no point in attempting to build the first GCS. Thus the designers concentrated on creating the biggest, noisiest and most powerful GCS the world had ever seen.

Its specifications called for a supersonic beam that would smash dentures in a 100-mile swath from Bangor to Chula Vista in only 43 minutes; a noise level twice that of the Jefferson Airplane; and atmospheric emissions guaranteed to bring on a new Ice Age.

Congress, flags waving, quickly appropriated another $1.2 billion for a prototype. After years of failures and set-backs, the first American GCS was unveiled on the grounds of the Washington Monument.

"This shows, my friends," said the President happily, "what we Americans can accomplish when we are faced, in my opinion, with a great challenge. As I push this button on this historic occasion, let me say that . . ."

Unfortunately, when the President pushed the button starting the GCS, the rest of his historic remarks could not, of course, be heard. But there was no question the GCS worked. And the spectators, from their glassy-eyed looks, were clearly deeply impressed.

At this point, a little boy at the edge of the throng cupped his hands to his mother's ear and shouted: "Who needs it?" She frowned and asked the man next to her. The question fanned out through the crowd and eventually spread across the Nation.

After much deliberation, the President announced to thunderous applause that now America had proved its leadership in crockery smashing, he was throwing the GCS into the sea. The French, the British and the Russians, after much discussion, followed suit.

Relative peace and quiet returned to the earth.

It was then, unfortunately, that word reached Washington the Russians were developing a Giant Garbage Maker (GGM) that would treble overnight the Soviet garbage output and . . .

An Interview With a Dinosaur

"Dinosaurs dominated the world during the Mesozoic era—from about 200 million years ago to about 60 million years ago . . . Scientists have advanced many reasons to explain why the dinosaurs died out"—The World Book Encyclopedia.

"Good morning, sir. You are a dinosaur?"

"Yes, I'm a brontosaurus myself. Come from a long line of brontosauri. We've lived here in this swamp for—oh—140 million years or so. Lovely place, don't you think?"

"Very. I see that you eat these succulent looking reeds that grow in the shallows."

"Yes, they're the only thing I care for really."

"But I see, sir, that as you move about you seem to trample more reeds underfoot than you eat."

"Well, when you weigh in at 50 tons . . ."

"But aren't you concerned, sir, about destroying your food supply?"

"Not at all, young man. There have always been plenty of reeds to eat and there always will be—even though the swamp is a bit shallower."

"Shallower?"

"When I was a lad it came up to my shoulders. Now it's up to my hips. I suppose that's what's got the young ones all stirred up—that and the change in climate."

"The climate's changed, sir?"

"Yes, it's much less humid than when I was a boy. It's not the coolness that bothers you, you know, it's the lack of humidity."

"You said, sir, that the young were stirred up?"

"Oh, just a few wild-eyed radicals. They're going around shouting. 'The swamp's drying up! The swamp's drying up!' Sheer nonsense. There's always been a swamp and there always will be a swamp. No swamp! It's impossible for the saurian mind to conceive."

"They have a plan of action?"

"Nothing practical. They want us all to learn to eat those leaves growing on the bank. Leaves, mind you! Can't abide the stuff. Doesn't set well, don't you know?"

"But if, just by chance, the swamp *is* drying up. . . ."

"I'm not about to change my ways, young man. Reed-eating was good enough for my grandfather a billion times removed and it's certainly good enough for me!"

"But, Sir, you agree that the world is changing. And yet you say you will make no attempt to adapt to these new conditions. Aren't you afraid you will become extinct?"

"Extinct! Are you out of your mind, young man? There have always been dinosaurs and there always will be dinosaurs. After you've been ruling the world for 140 million years, there's one thing you know in your bones."

"What's that, sir?"

"The Good Lord created this planet solely for the enjoyment of us dinosaurs."

"The earliest examples of Homo sapiens date from about 300,000 B.C."—The World Book Encyclopedia.

3

Modern Living

And Who Needs It?

The Run-Away Machine

Once upon a time the people at Wonderfuland worshipped Efficiency. And over the years they labored to build a huge and ingenious Efficiency Machine.

It was the greatest machine the world had ever seen. And the most efficient, too.

Whereas it used to take a Wonderfulander an hour to wash the dishes, a day to hew a path or a week to build a wagon, The Efficiency Machine would turn out far superior products in one-eighteenth of the time.

From its spouts there poured a veritable treasure trove of disposable paper plates, concrete, automobiles, television sets, aspirin tablets and Ping-Pong balls.

The people were terribly, terribly proud of their Efficiency Machine. "It gives us whatever we want," they said, "along with the leisure time to enjoy life."

At least that's what they said at first.

But as the years passed, The Efficiency Machine grew bigger. The bigger it was, the more goods it could produce. And, as this was its only aim, it grew bigger. And Bigger. And BIGGER.

By now it was spewing forth more disposable plates than the people could dispose of, more concrete than there were mountain meadows to pave and more automobiles than there were parking places.

"Well," said the people frowning, "at least it gives us more time to enjoy life."

But, of course, by now The Efficiency Machine had befouled the streams (it didn't drink), polluted the air (it didn't breathe) and scraped away all the wildflowers (for it neither saw nor smelled).

The people began to grumble. "Why don't those in control of our wonderful Efficiency Machine do something?" they demanded. But nobody, it turned out, was in control.

You see, the Wonderfulanders, who used to work for themselves, now all worked for the Machine. And while each was nominally in control of his small or large part, none was in control of the whole.

So the people began to realize that what they had on their hands was a mindless, run-away machine.

The Conservatives demanded that it be slowed down. But there were no brakes. The Liberals demanded it be fixed. But there were no adequate tools. The Radicals demanded it be blown up. But the Machine had efficient defenses to take care of the likes of them.

One wise man, Charles Reich, pointed out that the Machine produced only what the people wanted. So, if people would only want less, it would produce less.

Unfortunately, while it proved easy to convince the man with two cars that he didn't want three, it was hard to persuade the man with none that he didn't want one.

"After all," each man said, "what does one more car or paper plate or Ping-Pong ball matter?"

Then it was too late. The Machine, to be more efficient, produced a Thinking Machine, which the scientists understood.

It, in turn, produced a better Thinking Machine, which a few scientists understood. And it, in turn, produced an even better Thinking Machine, which no one understood.

And these machines, being dedicated solely to Efficiency like all machines, produced at last a Totally Efficient World.

In it, there was no grass nor trees, no grief nor joy, no tears nor laughter—and, of course, no human beings. For, as any machine will tell you, they're the most inefficient things of all.

Moral: Efficiency is a great help in getting you where you're going—if you know where you're going.

Nobody's Perfect, Bunny Lovers

When it comes to the grave problems America faces, the gravest is neither pollution, urban sprawl nor excess stomach acidity. It is Playboy magazine.

Never since the Marquis de Sade has any literary figure spread more pain and misery than Playboy's publisher, Hugh Hefner.

Statistics show that 68.3 per cent of young American males study one or more centerfold "Playmates of the Month" during their formative years. For hours on end.

"Aha," cries the young man, "so this is what young ladies look like without their clothes on! I'll find one for me." And he starts hunting.

The problem, of course, is that this isn't what young ladies look like without their clothes on at all. Not even young Playmate ladies.

An article in the new magazine, Audience, points out that after the painstakingly-selected Playmate is paid $5000 to take off her clothes, she is carefully posed so she doesn't wrinkle, sag or droop.

Thousands of studio shots are taken under ideal lighting conditions. One single print is chosen. Then even this best of all possible photographs is—heaven help us—doctored!

For at this point, the article says, Hefner steps in with his retouchers: "Take off the hair on her upper lip!" he orders. "Clean up the shadows around her underarms!"

It is this blatant dishonesty that causes such untold suffering. There is our young man. He has found the girl of his dreams. She looks, with her clothes on, like a Playmate with her clothes on.

Eagerly he marries her. Expectantly he swoops her off on a honeymoon—only to discover that she, like all human beings, occasionally wrinkles, sags, droops and/or exhibits downy lips or underarm shadow. Moreover, she doesn't even have a staple in her navel.

Is it any wonder that 68.3 per cent of American males go through life feeling cheated and frustrated? Is it any wonder that 17 out of 18 marriages today end in uxoricide, divorce or shouting matches. ("Why can't you take the hair off your upper lip? Clean up your underarm shadow!")

To save America from slowly drowning in this sea of domestic acrimony, a group of us humanitarians has brought out a new magazine called Realboy.

The centerfold "Realmate of the Month" in our first issue is Miss Elvira McGorkle, a 47-year-old unemployed fry cook from Bixby Falls, Mont. Miss McGorkle, who is 5-foot-2, weighs 175 pounds and has led a hard life, is depicted standing against a brightly-lit wall in the Bixby Falls Medical Clinic, all prepared for a free chest X-ray.

As we say in the caption, "It is a realmate like Miss McGorkle who makes American men appreciate their wives."

We are convinced that once Realboy replaces Playboy as the leader in its field, American males will grow up rational and sane.

No longer will they be obsessed by unattainable visions of perfection. No longer will they be pandered to by books, movies and advertising that prey upon their frustrations. At last they will accept marital sex for the good thing it is—an act of love between two imperfect humans.

At last they will accept reality.

We, the publishers of Realboy, ask no high rewards from a grateful nation for restoring its sanity. We only wish we could find some guy who'd buy a copy.

The Simple Life and How to Avoid It

Once upon a time, there was a busy, frustrated man named Henry D. Thoreaubach who yearned, like most of us, for the simple life.

Henry's life was very complicated. At the office, he spent half his time deciding whom to saddle with the problems he'd been saddled with. The other half was devoted to seeing people he didn't want to see, phoning people he didn't want to phone, and writing people he wished would drop dead.

Being a busy man, he had many labor-saving devices. He had machines to chew up his garbage, wash his dishes, entertain his children, launder his clothes and brush his teeth. His hobby was laboring to repair them. It was very time-consuming.

But he loved his family. And he tried to schedule 12-minute chats with his children at 6:18 p.m. daily and a romantic evening with his wife every other Wednesday—when he could squeeze them in.

Yet, somehow, Henry had the feeling he wasn't getting anywhere.

Well, one day Henry happened to read Thoreau's "Walden" during his Great Books Reading Hour (every third Tuesday, 9 to 10 p.m.). "That," he cried, "is the life for me!"

So he chucked his job, sold his house, bought an axe, ten pounds of nails and some fishhooks and set off to build a little log cabin in the wilderness.

He was lucky to find a nice 50-foot lot on a pond for only $19,500. And after he'd signed the mortgage, searched the title and assumed his pro-rata share of the bonded indebtedness for streets and sewers, it was his.

Then he shouldered his axe and went off to chop down a tree. Unfortunately, the Forest Service caught him. So after he paid his fine, he had to contract with the E-Z Credit Lumber Co. to deliver the logs. But he forgot a building permit.

The Building Inspector demanded studs on 16-inch centers. The Plumbing Inspector demanded enlarged toilet drains. The Electrical Inspector demanded No. 218a conduits. The Health Inspector . . . And when he tried to catch fish for his dinner he was socked $50 for failing to carry a license.

That's when Henry said the hell with it, returned to the city and went on welfare. Here was the simple life he'd yearned for. He didn't do a thing all day long. "I am no longer busy and frustrated," said Henry after two months of it, "I am bored and frustrated."

Fortunately, Henry got a job making umbrellas. Red ones, blue ones, flowered ones. He liked making umbrellas. People needed them. Besides, he didn't have to see people, phone people or write people he didn't want to see, phone or write. So he had lots of time on his hands.

He had time to picnic with his family, learn to play the piccolo, read "Catch 22" in a single sitting, master Urdu, take long walks and, oh, a jillion other things. In fact, he didn't have any time at all. His life was soon twice as busy and complicated as it ever was.

But Henry didn't care. He was very, very happy.

Moral: Life isn't simple these days. So why clutter it up with a lot of nonsense?

Aristotle and Jaki

Presenting . . .

ARISTOTLE AND JAKI
(A GREEK TRAGEDY)

Scene: A palace in a distant land, far from the sun-drenched Peloponnesian shores. The Chorus stands stage right. Aristotle and Jaki meet stage center.

Chorus: O, did mighty Aristotle, hero of the Greeks,
Defy the gods and dark-browed Callas,
To spirit home to his native Greece,
Fair Jaki, high priestess of her far-off land—
Just as proud Paris years before
Did carry fair Helen off to Troy,
Thus unleashing awesome Mars, who saw
Ten thousand Greeks and Trojans fall
Before the gates of Troy in armor-rattling war.
So, too, did Jaki's people
Rend their garments and tear their hair
And moan their fate on hearing of the news,
As the two lovers cleft the wine-dark sea
Aboard his ill-omened ship, Christina.
But, heartsore for her native land,
Fair Jaki has returned and now displays
For mighty Aristotle her humble palace.
Watch! For the hubris of these lovers—
Like proud Paris and fair Helen—
Shall once again unleash the gods of war.

Aristotle: Hark! I hear the clash of arms nearby in the night.

Jaki: It's only your servants fighting with my servants as usual. And I do wish you could learn to speak better English. Half of what you say is Greek to me.

Aristotle: Sorry. But they wouldn't fight so much if you'd tell your maids to stop going around red-eyed and humming "Camelot." And then with only four servant bedrooms in this place . . .

Jaki: There you go, throwing it up to me again that I married you for your money. What good's your money? Those wishy-washy bodyguards you hired can't block like the Secret Service. I got trapped in the lobby again today. And to think people are whispering that I married an old man for his money.

Aristotle (indignantly): Old? Who's old? Why, 63 isn't old.

Jaki: You're 68 and you know it. Even Teddy isn't speaking to me. He says if he gets introduced as "Aristotle's brother-in-law" one more time . . .

Aristotle (placatingly): Come, come, my pet. Let us make up and I will buy you any treasure you wish.

Jaki: Good. I'll take a new yacht. To think I have to cruise on that scruffy old Christina where Callas . . .

Aristotle: Now don't bring her into it. There was nothing between us.

Jaki: Look me in the eye and say that. Here, stand on a footstool. And another thing, why can't we live in my country?

Aristotle (angrily): Your country? You don't even own it. No, we'll go back to my country. And furthermore . . .

Chorus: And thus does every marriage,
From before the times of Troy,
Lead inevitably to war.
For the rich are brothers to the poor;
They do but fight over more costly things.

A Man's Home Is His Fortress

"Well, now, you must be Mrs. Throkimer. I'm George Grommet and I'll be happy to show you around Peaceful Dell Acres. As we like to say, 'We don't just sell homes at Peaceful Dell, we sell peace of mind.'

"Please don't touch that fence, folks, It's got 220,000 volts running through it.

"Now if you'll just show the guard here some identification—your birth certificate, passport, anything like that. Fine, fine. Now watch close. The guard puts his key in over there and I put a key in over here and—upsy-daisy!—there goes the portcullis. Great idea requiring two keys. We got it from the Minuteman Missile security program.

"Okay, folks, just step right in. Welcome to Peaceful Dell. If you'll just pause a minute in front of the x-ray machine here. Fine. Now turn sideways. Fine. No weapons. Not that we thought you'd be carrying any—ha, ha. Just routine for all arrivals.

"Now we'll just cross over the moat here. I wouldn't put my hand in, Mrs. Throkimer, if I were you. Those piranha are mighty mean. Just another precaution to make you feel more secure.

"Speaking of security precautions, Mr. Throkimer'll be interested in some of the little things we do here at Peaceful Dell to ease your mind.

"Now you see those guard towers on top of the inner wall? They're manned around the clock and those searchlights are going all night long. And maybe you noticed that plowed strip 50-foot wide as you came in. Claymore mines. Now, inside, we've got a 24-hour armored car patrol that . . . Look out, here comes one now. They can't see too well through those little slits.

"But I'll bet you Mrs. Throkimer wants to see one of our Peaceful Dell homes. I know how the ladies are, always thinking about the nest while us men folks are thinking about protection.

"Let's see, I think I'll show you the Melvin place first. You'll like that. It's handy to the Commissary and the Exercise Yard.

"Here we are. Now you'll notice, Mr. Throkimer, that the walls are solid concrete, four feet thick. You could hit those walls with a dozen Molotov cocktails and hardly scratch the surface.

"Now, I'll just get the door open here. Let's see, 42 left, 13 right, 27 left. We'll have the combination changed for you, of course. Can you give me a hand pushing it open, Mr. Throkimer? That's solid steel, 18 inches thick.

"And let me point out one feature of this door that no other tract offers. A time lock. It can't be opened from inside or out from 9 p.m. to 6 a.m. That protects you from accidentally wandering out on the streets and getting shot during curfew.

"Now, Mrs. Throkimer, just you look around and see all the modern conveniences—air purifier, underground water supply, a larder big enough for three tons of canned goods. Why, you could hold out here for six months.

"And let me tell you, folks, that this place is a steal. Belonged to old Mike Melvin. Lived here alone for seven years. Then one night he shot a guard while trying to break out of here after dark.

"The judge ruled him legally sane. But I got my doubts. He sure is an odd one. I had a letter from him the other day from Leavenworth. He says it's just like home."

A Fighting Christian Gospel

In these days of wars and riots, with neighbors arming themselves against neighbors, good Christians naturally turn to The Bible for comfort.

Undoubtedly, good Christians can find the greatest comfort these days in that little known Book of The Bible, "The Gospel According to St. Pontius."

There is nothing to make a man feel more comfortable these days, good Christians agree, than going out, buying a gun, stocking up on ammunition and curling up with St. Pontius. Chapter and verse follow.

And seeing the multitudes, he went up into a mountain: and when his disciples came unto him, he taught them, saying,

Blessed are the proud in spirit, for no man shall dare trifle with them.

Blessed are the self-righteous, for their aim shall not waver.

Blessed are the well-to-do, for they shall be thrice-armed and with better weapons.

Blessed are the peacemakers, particularly the Colt .44.

And I say unto you, whosoever shall smite thee on the right cheek, counter with a left hook.

Ye have heard that it hath been said, thou shalt love thy neighbor and hate thine enemy. But I say unto you, How do you know you can trust thy neighbor?

And it came to pass that when he had ended his Sermon on the Mount and was come down from the mountain, great multitudes followed him. And he organized them into companies and battalions and regiments, saying unto them,

Render unto God that which is God's. And, having done

that, render Caesar's soldiers wherever you catch them.

After this manner therefore pray ye: Our Father which art in heaven, Hallowed be thy name. Give us this day revenge upon our enemies. Forgive us our tactical errors and lead us not into ambushes, but deliver us an encouraging body count.

Strengthen our arms so that we may smite the enemy hip and thigh and bless our swords so that they may drink deep of his blood in the righteousness of our cause. For ours will be this kingdom, and the power, and the glory, forever. Amen.

And, lo, his prayers were granted and he became a great General, slaughtering the enemy by the thousands and destroying their cities and laying waste to the countryside.

And he grew rich in years and honors: Founder of the Judea First Committee, Executive Secretary of the Aramaic Citizens Councils, and Honorary Commander of the Nazareth Minutemen.

And on his death bed he called his Disciples unto him, saying, Go ye forth to all nations, teaching them that they shalt not kill, except on orders of a superior officer, in self defense or to get even.

And then he spake prophecy, saying, And they who shall follow in this path shall be known as Good Christians, even unto the end of the world. Amen.

And, lo, so it came to pass.

The Strangest Planet of All

The star ship, NX8307, Captain Xenon commanding, returned safely to her home base on Arcturus IV and the Captain, looking somewhat nervous, strode to the Council of Wise Elders to make his report.

"Well, Captain," said the Eldest Elder, "did you find a planet we might colonize and exploit?"

"I think so, sir," said Captain Xenon uneasily. "Terra, the third planet out from Sol. A lovely green world. True, the atmosphere is thick with carbon monoxide, but breathable. The waters are turgid with pollutants, but purifiable. And the inhabitants are bellicose and a little mad, but basically lovable."

"It sounds colonizable, Captain. But is it exploitable? What do these natives make?"

"Money, sir. From the cradle to the grave, the primary drive of each native is to make as much money as possible."

"Ah," said the Eldest Elder, "they have discovered a precious asset worth striving for. Tell us, Captain, what is money?"

Here the Captain frowned. "It's a little difficult to explain, sir."

"Come, come, Captain. Is it edible, drinkable, wearable, lethal or purely aesthetic?"

"No, sir. It's . . . Well, it's pieces of paper."

"Paper, Captain?"

"Yes sir. They toil, lie, cheat, steal, kill and war for it. But that's because it represents gold."

"Oh yes, that soft, yellow metal. They've found some use for gold, other than filling teeth?"

"No, sir. It's intrinsically worthless, too, but they dig it up out of the ground and then bury it under the ground. They believe this makes the pieces of paper valuable."

"Just a minute, Captain . . ."

"At the moment, sir, the whole planet is in crisis because the leading nation state has less worthless gold buried under ground than it used to have, and they fear this may make the worthless paper money worthless, in which case millions will starve because . . .

"Control yourself, please, Captain."

". . . because each native values the paper only because all other natives value it. And should their faith in this worthless paper be destroyed, they would stop producing food, clothing and shelter because they'd have nothing worthless to strive for and . . ."

At this point, Captain Xenon had to be forcibly restrained. And he was led off babbling something about 35 pieces of paper per ounce, Arab sheiks, General de Gaulle, seven bankers, dual pricing, gold pools and other hallucinatory nonsense.

The Council of Wise Elders then voted unanimously to bypass Terra and instead colonize Betelgeuse XIV, where the mauve-colored three-headed inhabitants devoted their lives to making pistachio ice cream.

"When it comes to money," said the Eldest Elder wisely, "let's take pistachio."

Sex Rites of the Ugulaps

Herewith is another stimulating chapter from that anthropological study, "Strange Sex Rites Among The Ugulap Savages." Unfortunately, this chapter deals not with sex rites, but with the weird custom these backward natives have of staring at rocks.

In the center of each native hut stands a roughly-hewn rock two or three feet square. It is apparently a votive shrine to the most powerful of all the gods in the pantheon of these superstitious savages.

For while the Ugulaps pay passing homage to various fertility symbols, miscellaneous demons and other primitive deities, their devotions to the rock consume literally hours of their time each day.

The ritual begins in each hut as the sun goes down. The family gathers on one side of the rock in a semi-circle. The mother places the evening meal on the lap of each family member. Mother, father and children then turn to stare at the flat, gray, dull surface of the rock.

It is then that a peculiar psychic phenomenon occurs: Each family member goes into a mindless trance.

The trance lasts from two to six hours. Communication is limited to monosyllabic grunts. While under the spell, the natives can perform simple motor activities, but they do so with reluctance.

For example, after several hours the mother will arise to put the protesting children to bed. Or the father will periodically exit to pour himself another gourd of "boing!"—the native malt brew. But they return to the rock as quickly as possible to resume staring at it as a bird stares at a snake.

The purpose of this rigorous daily ritual is far from clear. The natives apparently feel that the rock will some day magically confer on them wisdom and enlightenment.

"What did you see on the rock last night?" they will occasionally ask each other the next day. But the answer is invariably, "Nothing much." And yet they persist with an endurance that defies the imagination.

Naturally, the children are trained from infancy in rock watching. By the age of eight, most can sit motionless in front of a rock for 12 hours at a stretch, their blank minds extremely susceptible to suggestion.

It is little wonder, then, that they hallucinate, envisioning figures of clowns, medicine men and talking rabbits. The function of these imaginary creatures, oddly enough, is to tell the children what to eat.

Ten times each hour, on the average, one of these fantasies orders the poor, unthinking child to consume a bowl of "krunchi-wunchi," "snax-smax" or other dubious native dishes—all of them syrupy sweet and of little nutritional value. It is these hypnotic suggestions, driven home over and over, that of course shape the natives' dietary habits through life.

Yet the Ugulap mother, being untutored, not only approves of her child's day-long rock watching (it keeps the youngster out of mischief), but cares little about even rudimentary nutrition.

Thus, it is no surprise that the Ugulaps grow up with rotten teeth, flabby muscles, pot bellies and virtually blank minds. After all, such attributes make for ideal rock watchers.

Fortunately, however, help is on the way. A television antenna even now is being erected on Ugulap Island to bring education, entertainment and all the blessings of this modern electronic miracle to these poor, uncivilized savages.

The Murder of Grabwell Grommet

On the morning of his 42nd birthday, Grabwell Grommet awoke to a peal of particularly ominous thunder. Glancing out the window with bleary eyes, he saw written in fiery letters across the sky:

"SOMEONE IS TRYING TO KILL YOU, GRABWELL GROMMET!"

With shaking hands, Grommet lit his first cigarette of the day. He didn't question the message. You don't question messages like that. His only question was, "Who?"

At breakfast as he salted his fried eggs, he told his wife, Gratia, "Someone's trying to kill me."

"Who?" she asked with horror.

Grommet slowly stirred the cream and sugar into his coffee and shook his head. "I don't know," he said.

Convinced though he was, Grommet couldn't go to the police with such a story. He decided his only course was to go about his daily routine and hope somehow to outwit his would-be murderer.

He tried to think on the drive to the office. But the frustrations of making time by beating lights and switching lanes occupied him wholly.

Nor, once behind his desk, could he find a moment, what with jangling phones, urgent memos and the problems and decisions piling up as they did each day.

It wasn't until his second martini at lunch that the full terror of his position struck him. It was all he could do to finish his Lasagna Milanese.

"I can't panic," he said to himself, lighting his cigar. "I

simply must live my life as usual."

So he worked till seven as usual. Drove home fast as usual. Had his two cocktails as usual. Ate a hearty dinner as usual. Studied business reports as usual. And took his usual two Seconal capsules in order to get his usual six hours sleep.

As the days passed, he manfully stuck to his routine. And as the months went by, he began to take a perverse pleasure in his ability to survive.

"Whoever's trying to get me," he'd say proudly to his wife, "hasn't got me yet. I'm too smart for him."

"Oh, please be careful," she'd reply, ladling him a second helping of Beef Stroganoff.

The pride grew as he managed to go on living for years. But, as it must to all men, death came at last to Grabwell Grommet. It came at his desk on a particularly busy day. He was 53.

His grief-striken widow demanded a full autopsy.

But it showed only emphysema, arteriosclerosis, duodenal ulcers, cirrhosis of the liver, cardiac necrosis, a cerebrovascular aneurism, pulmonary edema, obesity, circulatory insufficiency and a touch of lung cancer.

"How glad Grabwell would have been to know," said the widow, smiling proudly through her tears, "that he died of natural causes."

The Game of Life

Once upon a time, there were four brothers. Their names were Midas, Caesar, Whitfellow and George. Each was ambitious in his own way.

"I want to be rich," said Midas.

"I want to be powerful," said Caesar.

"I want to be famous," said Whitfellow.

"I guess," said George, "I just want to be happy."

And each was.

Midas became a businessman. He plunged here, held back there and by the time he was 30, he was a millionaire.

While a million was more than Midas could ever spend, naturally he didn't stop there. Making money was too exciting. It was his whole life. So he merged here and consolidated there and finally he was a millionaire 272 times over!

He was understandably gratified to read on his death bed: "End Near for Country's Richest Man."

Caesar went into politics. It was very exciting. He wheeled and dealed and by the time he was 30, he was Mayor of his city.

While he had more power as Mayor than he could use, Caesar naturally didn't stop there. Acquiring power was too exciting. It was his whole life. So he gambled and parlayed and finally he became the power behind the throne!

He was understandably gratified on his death bed to read: "End Near for Country's Most Powerful Man."

Whitfellow went on the stage. It was very exciting. He acted and recited and emoted and by the time he was 30, he was applauded by thousands.

While the applause of thousands was enough to fill any theater, Whitfellow naturally didn't stop there. Seeking fame was too exciting. It was his whole life. So he went into the movies and onto television and finally he was internationally renowned!

He was understandably gratified to read on his death bed: "End Near for Country's Most Famous Man."

As for George, nothing much ever happened to him. Like most of us, he had no more money than he could use, only a single vote in every election and hardly a stranger knew his name.

But he had a job he liked, played tennis every Wednesday and Saturday, married a wonderful girl and had three fine children. That was his whole life. But he was happy—even though on his death bed there wasn't a word in the papers.

When the brothers entered Heaven, the other three were a trifle annoyed at George. "You may have found happiness," they said, frowning, "but what have you got to show for your life other than three tarnished tennis trophies?"

"Well, no offense," said George, "but other men were richer than you, Midas; other men more powerful than you, Caesar; and, Whitfellow, 2 billion people on earth never heard of your name."

"But if you had sought riches or power or fame," they said, angrily, "you would have had the excitement that comes with winning or losing."

"Personally," said George with a smile, "I preferred tennis."

Moral: It isn't whether you win or lose, it's whether you know what game you're playing.

Ban the Bomb Banners

The recent wave of legislation in Congress to curb bombings has stirred up a hornet's nest. Whipping up protest is the huge and influential National Bomb Association.

The NBA's motto, which can been seen on the bumpers of pickup trucks and campers across the land, is, of course:

"WHEN BOMBS ARE OUTLAWED, ONLY OUTLAWS WILL HAVE BOMBS."

The NBA's case is most thoughtfully set forth in the November issue of the organization's magazine, "The National Bomber." The cover depicts a kindly, pipe-smoking father showing his grinning, freckle-faced son how to light the fuse of a small, junior-sized stick of TNT.

The lead article is entitled simply: "WHO Is Behind This Plot to Take Away the Only Means We Americans Have to Defend Our Homes, Our Families and Our Flag?" Excerpts follow.

Bombs (writes the author, J. B. (Buck) Buckley are as American as apple pie. They are part of our heritage, our history and, bursting in air, our National Anthem.

Let us ne'er forget that the inalienable people's right to bear bombs and other arms is guaranteed by our sacred Constitution itself. In their wisdom, our Founding Fathers foresaw that America would ne'er remain free without bombs.

What war would we have ever won without bombs? Without bombs, America would long since have been overrun by the British, the Mexicans, the Spanish, the Huns, the Nips, the Nazis, the North Koreans and the Viet Cong.

Instead, thanks to early training of our Nation's youth

under NBA-sponsored programs, we have preserved our heritage of having the finest bombers in the world.

It's bombing in the Great Outdoors that holds the family together. What Dad's heart hasn't swelled with pride to see the look in his boy's eyes after the lad has bombed his first rabbit with a well-thrown hand grenade? Show me the kid who's out bombing ducks in the crisp autumn air and I'll show you a kid who isn't hanging around a pool hall smoking marijuana.

But now they would take our bombs away from us. First, they would curtail our right to purchase bombs through the mail. Next they would license every bomber in the land. And lastly, they would force us to get permits from some faceless bureaucrat to keep bombs in the sanctity of our very own homes.

It seems clear this is a calculated plot. Once they have cut off our supplies, once they have our names on a list, once they know where every single bomb is in this great land of ours, they will swoop down in the night, seize our weapons and render us defenseless.

Who is behind this plot? Simply ask yourself, "Who wants to render America defenseless at home and abroad?"

And what excuse do the tools of this conspiracy offer for their vicious legislation? "Bombs," they say, "are dangerous."

But it's a known fact that more people are killed each year with paring knives than with bombs. Yet do they propose to outlaw paring knives? As we of the NBA say:

"Bombs don't kill people, only people kill people!"

So let every loyal American join in preserving our precious freedom to bear bombs. For in these perilous times, can any American sleep easily at night, knowing he is safe from harm, unless he has a bomb under his bed?

Ne'er!

The Best of All Worlds

Once upon a time there was a goodhearted man named Mark Hawkins, who strove to make this the best of all possible worlds.

He eagerly picketed for peace. He enthusiastically jousted for justice. He ebulliently bled for brotherhood. And though he lived a long and rich and exciting life, peace and justice and brotherhood seemed little closer than before.

At last, as all men must, Mr. Hawkins came to The Pearly Gates. The fire of battle was in his eye.

"Hand me a picket sign!" he cried to The Gatekeeper. "To the barricades! Now that I've finally reached the Power Center, we'll push through great and sweeping changes to make Earth the best of all possible worlds."

"Something wrong?" asked The Gatekeeper, nervously adjusting his halo.

"Good grief!" said Mr. Hawkins. "Earth is a living hell of war, injustice and intolerance. Yet if we all pitched in, it could so easily be a veritable heaven."

"Earth- Hmmm. Earth," said The Gatekeeper, scratching his flowing white beard. "Wait till I get down my Book of E's. I'll check."

"Check?" Mr. Hawkins was startled. "You mean you don't . . ."

"There's million-trillion worlds, you know," said The Gatekeeper, testily. "No two alike. Can't keep track of them all. Ah, here we are. E . . . A. Did you say 'Eard?' No, you couldn't be from Eard. At their request we granted them eternal life a billion or so years ago."

"What a magnificent gift! How did it turn out?"

"Musty. Very musty. For the past nine hundred million years they've been working to invent death. An impossibility, of course. Now here's Earfram. Lovely planet. They demanded eternal peace two eons ago. We gave it to them."

"Eternal peace! There's a cause to fight for. Are they happy?"

"It's hard to tell. They just lie around with their eyes somewhat glazed. Next comes Earghop. Now that was an interesting experiment. We decided to grant them every single thing they asked for."

"Everything? You mean justice and brotherhood, too?"

"And freedom from want, disease, toil, smog, taxes, Excedrin headaches . . . In fact we solved every single one of their problems."

"Now that must be the best of all possible worlds. Are they gloriously happy?"

"No, they're dead. They all died off in 52 years."

"My goodness! What did they die of?"

"Boredom. Wait, here we are. Earth. Ah, yes, we did supply you with one—the only one—precious gift. You can see the entry here: 'Granted to Earth, in The Beginning—One (1) bootstrap.' "

The puzzled frown left Mr. Hawkins' face and he smiled gently. "I see," he said.

"But it's no concern of yours any more," said The Gatekeeper, putting away the book of E's. "For now you enter Heaven, there to dwell in eternal peace, all your problems behind you, your every request granted."

"Oh, I have just one."

"What's that?"

"Please, Sir," said Mr. Hawkins, squaring his shoulders, thrusting forth his jaw and the old lively gleam of battle returning once more to his eye, "Can I go to Hell?"

Moral: This is the best of all possible worlds.

The End of the Stock Market

New York, June 12, 1972—
The Dow Jones Industrial Average closed at minus 18 today and the New York Stock Exchange was converted into a Federal Bingo Parlor.

The end of the stock market as an economic institution had been predicted by some experts ever since the averages hit zero last month.

At the time, however, many leaders expressed confidence that the downward trend was over.

"I believe the market has definitely found a new base," said Chesney McMartin, the third Federal Reserve Board Chairman in the past three weeks.

"If I had any money," said President Nixon, on being advised that all stocks were now worthless, "I'd be buying stocks right now."

Unfortunately, the market, which had been dropping at the rate of more than one point a day since Mr. Nixon's Inauguration, continued to do just that.

Most economists contended that the zero level was "a psychological barrier" to further price drops.

Investors, however, found few buyers willing to take their stock off their hands, even for nothing. "Who wants a bunch of worthless stocks?" was the cry from both sides.

The market broke through the zero level the following day. Experts blamed "the lack of encouraging news" and explained the market had nowhere to go but down as "it sought new levels."

General Motors closed at minus two and a quarter—meaning a seller had to pay a buyer $22.50 to take ten shares. Stockholders, worried about the growing liability their shares now represented, drove the market down farther in the week that followed.

The President again expressed confidence. "If I needed any money," he said, "I'd be buying stocks right now."

What has saved the economy has been the gradualness of the decline—so unlike the crash of '29.

As long ago as the spring of 1970, stockholders, brokers and the public had grown accustomed to seeing the market sag one to twenty points a day with a few brief rallies. Thus there was no panic as in '29.

The public, unafraid of a depression, continued investing in new businesses and creating new jobs. Indeed, inflation, rather than depression, has remained the problem with prices going up as the market went down.

This clear demonstration that the stock market had no relationship to the economy—nor, some suspected, to reality—led to passage of The Bingo Bill.

The bill, of course, abolishes the stock market and establishes in its stead a National Bingo Game.

There was some opposition from churches which complained of "unfair government competition" with their free enterprise system. But the bill sailed through Congress—its sponsors easily proving that in Bingo the rules were more orderly, the odds more predictable and the rewards more gratifying than in the stock market.

"At least in Bingo," said one Senator, hammering home the chief selling point, "somebody wins."

And so the President opened the first Federal Bingo Parlor here today in appropriate ceremonies.

"If I had any money," he said confidently as he cut the ribbon, "I'd play Bingo."

How to Stay Alive

Once upon a time there was a man named Snadley Klabberhorn who was the healthiest man in the whole wide world.

Snadley wasn't always the healthiest man in the whole wide world. When he was young, Snadley smoked what he wanted, drank what he wanted, ate what he wanted, and exercised only with young ladies in bed.

He thought he was happy. "Life is absolutely peachy," he was fond of saying. "Nothing beats being alive."

Then along came the Surgeon General's Report linking smoking to lung cancer, heart disease, emphysema and tertiary coreopsis.

Snadley read about The Great Tobacco Scare with a frown. "Life is so peachy," he said, "that there's no sense taking any risks." So he gave up smoking.

Like most people who went through the hell of giving up smoking, Snadley became more interested in his own health. In fact, he became fascinated. And when he read a WCTU tract which pointed out that alcohol caused liver damage, brain damage and acute weltanschauung, he gave up alcohol and drank dietary colas instead.

At least he did until The Great Cyclamate Scare.

"There's no sense taking any risks," he said. And he switched to sugar-sweetened colas, which made him fat and caused dental caries. On realizing this he renounced colas in favor of milk and took up jogging, which was an awful bore.

That was about the time of The Great Cholesterol Scare.

Snadley gave up milk. To avoid cholesterol, which caused atherosclerosis, coronary infarcts and chronic chryselephantinism, he also gave up meat, fats and dairy products, subsisting on a diet of raw fish.

Then came The Great DDT Scare.

"The presence of large amounts of DDT in fish . . ." Snadley read with anguish. But fortunately that's when he met Ernestine. They were made for each other. Ernestine introduced him to home-ground wheat germ, macrobiotic yogurt and organic succotash.

They were very happy eating this dish thrice daily, watching six hours of color television together and spending the rest of their time in bed.

They were, that is, until The Great Color Television Scare.

"If color tee-vee does give off radiations," said Snadley, "there's no sense taking risks. After all, we still have each other."

And that's about all they had. Until The Great Pill Scare.

On hearing that The Pill might cause carcinoma, thromboses and lingering stichometry, Ernestine promptly gave up The Pill—and Snadley. "There's no sense taking any risks," she said.

Snadley was left with his jogging. He was until he read somewhere that 1.3 per cent of all joggers are eventually run over by a truck or bitten by rabid dogs.

He then retired to a bomb shelter in his back yard (to avoid being hit by a meteor), installed an air purifier (after The Great Smog Scare) and spent the next 63 years doing Royal Canadian Air Force exercises and poring over back issues of The Reader's Digest.

"Nothing's more important than being alive," he said proudly on reaching 102. But he never did say anymore that life was absolutely peachy.

CAUTION: Being alive may be hazardous to your health.

Christians Are in the Minority

Scene: The Heavenly Real Estate Office. The Landlord, humming a little tune, is happily whipping up another galaxy to place in the firmament as his agent, Mr. Gabriel, enters hesitantly.

The Landlord: And now if I take a million parsecs of stardust, add a billion bushels of moonglow, stir thoroughly and . . .

Gabriel: Excuse me, sir. But you did ask that I interrupt you with any reports from Earth.

The Landlord: Earth? Oh, yes, that lovely little green planet I made. Such a gem. (frowning) More trouble, I suppose.

Gabriel: Yes, sir. Another fight's broken out. This time in Ireland.

The Landlord (with a smile): Ah, the Emerald Isle. One of the best examples of my handiwork, if I do say so myself. And the Irish. Confidentially, Gabriel, I can't help having a soft spot in my heart for the Irish. Such a warm, loving people.

Gabriel: Yes, sir, they are currently being bombed, shot, burned and clubbed.

The Landlord (sternly): Who risks my wrath by attacking my jolly, lovable Irish?

Gabriel: As usual, sir, the Irish.

The Landlord (thoughtfully): I think it's high time I personally intervened down there. I shall wisely adjudicate the dispute and thereby demonstrate how all men can live in peace and brotherhood.

Gabriel (nervously): Frankly, sir, I'd advise against that. The issues are rather difficult to . . .

The Landlord (annoyed): Are you doubting my omnipotence, Gabriel? Just tick off the facts and I'll hand down my verdict. Now, just why are the Irish beating and killing each other?

Gabriel: Well, basically, sir, to determine which are the better Christians.

The Landlord: I beg your pardon, Gabriel?

Gabriel: You see, sir, the Protestant majority has been persecuting the Catholic minority for years in Northern Ireland because the Catholics burn candles, eat wafers and drink wine in church.

The Landlord: Well, that's settled. Obviously, those who would persecute their fellow men for such piddling reasons have no concept of what Christianity is all about. I will declare the Catholics the true Christians and have done with it.

Gabriel: Yes, sir. Does that apply to the Catholic majorities in Spain, South America and elsewhere who have been persecuting Protestant minorities for years because they don't burn candles, eat wafers and drink wine in church?

The Landlord: Good me, no. Is that all they can do, persecute each other?

Gabriel: Oh, no, sir. They also persecute the Jews, Moslems, Hindus, Buddhists . . .

The Landlord (sadly): Are there no true Christians down there, Gabriel?

Gabriel: Well, the Jews have been so busy being persecuted over the centuries they haven't had much time to persecute anyone else. But if you want to declare them the true Christians, you'd better hurry, sir. Now that they have a Jewish State and an Arab minority . . . Perhaps, sir, it would be safer to declare that true Christians are always in the minority, whatever minority it might be. Sir? Are you listening?

The Landlord (self absorbed): And add a phantasmagoria of rainbows, one Milky Way, eight octaves of birdsong . . .

The Man Who Didn't Play the Market

Once upon a time there was a young man named Ainsley Bloor who was a good American in all things but one.

He was a good husband, a good provider and hit a good three wood. But he didn't play the stock market.

When friends chided him for his failure to invest in America, Ainsley blamed it on a flaw in his character. "Heck," he'd say apologetically, "I don't even shoot craps."

One day, Ainsley ran into an old high school chum named Wentworth who was a young securities salesman. "Buy Xero at 27," said Wentworth in a husky whisper.

"What does Xero make or do?" asked Ainsley.

"Who knows?" said Wentworth. "All I know is that it's going sky high."

"If you know whether a stock is going up or down, why aren't you rich?" inquired Ainsley out of curiosity and Wentworth never spoke to him again.

On arriving home that evening, Ainsley mentioned the incident in passing to his wife, Versillia, but she showed little interest. The next morning he couldn't help idly checking the price of Xero and noted with mild satisfaction that it had dropped a point to 26.

"Let's see," he said to Versillia at breakfast, "If we had taken our life savings of $2700 and bought 100 shares, we'd already have lost $100."

The following day Xero dropped another point and two more the day after that. "How about that?" said Ainsley happily. "We're $400 ahead!" Versillia went out and bought a new Queen Anne highboy.

In the weeks that followed Xero fell steadily and Ainsley could hardly wait to check the market quotations each day. The high point came when Xero hit a low of 17.

"The stock market's a wonderful thing," said Ainsley elatedly. "We haven't been in it six weeks and we're $1000 to the good." They began living beyond their means.

Then the market turned. Xero started climbing. "It's only a temporary adjustment," Ainsley kept saying with a worried frown. By January Xero was back at 27.

"We're even," said Versillia nervously. "Maybe we ought to buy in."

"I know what I'm doing!" growled Ainsley. "It's bound to go down again." But it went up.

Ainsley took to having two martinis before dinner and called brokers anonymously in mid-day to check Xero's movements. Still it climbed. He made Versillia take the Queen Anne highboy back and do her own hair.

On May 24, Xero reached 37. "We've lost $1000," said Ainsley with a piteous groan.

But the worst was yet to come. On a black Friday in October, Xero Soared to 54—double the original price. "That's $2700," cried Ainsley, his face as white as a sheet, "our entire life savings!"

With fumbling fingers, he took his revolver out of the night stand drawer, shot Versillia and put a bullet through his own head. In the note he left, he blamed the tragedy on "financial worries caused by my own rash judgment in not playing the stock market."

Moral: If the stock market crashes, it's going to make a lot of people happy.

The Crazy Ideas Of Grosbert Grommet

Scene: The offices of Dr. Zang Freud. Enter Mr. Grosbert Grommet, a shy, middle-aged man, and his wife, Grimelda, a big-boned woman with a sense of purpose.

Mrs. Grommet: Here he is, Doctor. Here's this lummox of a husband of mine. He's fruitier than a nutcake. You've got to put him away, Doctor. For his own good, mind you.

Mr. Freud: Please, Mrs. Grommet. First I'll have to ask him some questions to determine whether, as you say, he has actually lost contact with reality.

Mrs. Grommet: Hoo-boy! He can't tell reality from a hole in his head. Go ahead, ask him about the war.

Dr. Freud: Do you realize, Mr. Grommet, that we are engaged in a war?

Mr. Grommet (nervously): Oh, yes. We have dropped three million tons of napalm and high explosives on the inhabitants of a tiny Asian country in a war we now concede we will never win. But we will continue to bomb and shoot them.

Mrs. Grommet (eagerly): Tell him why, Grosbert.

Mr. Grommet (promptly): Because they want us to. We only want to do what they want us to do.

Mrs. Grommet: Hah! See, Doctor? He thinks somewhere there's a nation of masochists. And listen to this. How would you help the poor?

Mr. Grommet: By increasing unemployment. We must increase unemployment in order to have a stronger economy.

Mrs. Grommet: Such a nut I married! Now tell the Doctor about your fear of Chinese missiles.

Mr. Grommet: Oh, I'm not afraid of them any more. I

used to be. So I was willing to spend $5 billion on an anti-Chinese ballistic missile system to protect our cities. But that was silly. So, instead, I'm now for spending $8 billion on an anti-Russian ballistic missile system to protect our missiles. For years, they've been protected by a Cyclone fence.

Mrs. Grommet (slyly): Anti-Chinese missiles, Anti-Russian missiles. What's the difference between them Grosbert?

Mr. Grommet (shrugging): None whatsoever. I just call them by different names.

Mrs. Grommet (rubbing her hands): And finally, Grosbert, why did the Governor of California call out the National Guard?

Mr. Grommet: Because some people planted flowers and grass in a vacant lot. So we had to shoot and gas thousands of them because a few militants shouted obscenities and threw bricks at the police.

Mrs. Grommet (happily): And why do these militants shout obscenities and throw bricks?

Mr. Grommet: Same as always—to make this world a better place in which to live.

Mrs. Grommet (triumphantly to Dr. Freud): Hoo-hah! Is he ever off his rocker! Now will you sign the commitment papers, Doctor?

Dr. Freud: I already have, Mrs. Grommet. Guards!

(*Two men in white jackets enter, the Doctor points and, after a brief struggle, they lead out Mrs. Grommet.*)

Dr. Freud (shaking his head): Obviously she thinks that everyone, from our leaders on down, is insane. A clear case of paranoia, I'm afraid, Mr. Grommet.

Mr. Grommet: I would've warned her that anybody who doesn't keep up with current events these days is crazy. (with a little smile) But she never stopped talking.

A Fable for Labor Day

Once upon a time in Wonderfuland, the country was bitterly divided into two classes—the Workers and the Bosses.

The Bosses dwelt in marble palaces, never engaged in honest toil, made lots of money, controlled many of the nation's legislators, told their men where and when they could work, supported wars, hated radicals and said things like, "Let's not rock the boat."

They were terrible, stuffy old conservatives.

The Workers, on the other hand, lived in hovels, labored 60 hours a week for a pittance, controlled not even their own lives, loved peace, admired radicals and said things like, "All men are brothers."

They were wonderful, starry-eyed liberals.

And it seemed as though strife-torn Wonderfuland would never achieve equality, unity and tranquility.

But, fortunately, there arose among the Workers a brave new breed of men known as Labor Leaders. "Workers of the world unite," they cried. "And hit the bricks."

At first a few Workers flocked to their banners and then thousands. There were picket lines and protest demonstrations and sit-in strikes.

The Bosses looked out of the windows of their marble palaces. "Look at those dirty, long-haired, radical, unemployed bums," they said in abhorrence. "Call the cops."

So there were arrests and jailings and riots and strife, strife, strife. But slowly, as the years passed, the Labor Leaders grimly dragged one concession after another from the Bosses.

Eventually, the Workers only had to work half as long.

For four times the money. And each had a nice house and two cars and a color tee-vee and an electric shoe-polisher and free psychiatric care.

Nor did they complain about "exploitation by the Bosses" any more. Instead, they complained about "high property taxes" and "welfare chiselers."

As for the Labor Leaders, they built marble palaces to dwell in as befits those who run multi-million-dollar organizations. And they made lots of money. And they controlled many of the nation's legislators. And they told their men where and when they could work.

They still said, "All men are brothers." But they couldn't see much point in letting black-skinned or brown-skinned men in their organizations. "After all," they said, "let's not rock the boat."

Of course, there were still pickets and protest demonstrators and sit-ins. But most were protesting an inane war or racial inequality or some such new-fangled cause.

"Look at those dirty, long-haired, radical, unemployed bums," said the Labor Leaders in abhorrence as they looked out of the windows of their marble palaces. "Call the cops."

So at long last equality, unity and tranquility were restored in Wonderland—at least between the Workers and the Bosses.

"Imagine finding out after all these years of bitter struggle," as one Labor Leader put it over a three-martini lunch, "that you Bosses are just like us."

Moral: If you would really destroy a radical movement, let it win.

Coffee, Tea or Hemlock?

A battle is shaping up in Congress over hemlock advertising.

On one side are the anti-hemlock forces who cite a 1965 report by the Surgeon General showing that drinking hemlock causes people to topple over dead.

As a result, all hemlock bottles have since been required to carry the message on their labels: "Warning: Drinking hemlock may be hazardous to your health."

At issue now are plans by the FCC to force hemlock advertisers to include similar warnings in their television commercials—such as, "step up to the cool taste of hemlock, which may kill you." Or, "hemlock tastes good, like any lethal poison should."

The hemlock industry says it could not live with such stringent regulations.

Leading the battle for the industry is Representative Willie Snavehart of Georgia, whose district includes some of the nation's largest hemlock growers.

He has long pooh-poohed the 1965 findings of the Surgeon General's study that showed that of 123,246 males who ingested hemlock, 123,244 toppled over dead.

"Statistics can be used to prove anything," Congressman Snavehart said in a fighting speech on the floor of the House last week, "anything but the truth."

He then went on to cite statistics showing that any stricter regulations on the hemlock industry would cause "widespread economic deprivation and hardship on thousands upon thousands of little American hemlock growers who are the Backbone of our Nation."

He admitted that "some folks may topple over dead after drinking hemlock." But he said, "no direct link between hemlock drinking and toppling over dead has been scientifically proved." Thus, he said, "to blame hemlock drinking for folks toppling over dead is unfair, unscientific and un-American."

"The great American hemlock industry," he said "has more than met its responsibilities in this field by giving up claims that hemlock drinking makes you healthier."

As chairman of the powerful House Committee on Fiduciary Malpractice, Snavehart pushed through a bill forbidding any government agency from restricting any hemlock advertising anywhere. The Snavehart bill would prevent the FCC from banning hemlock advertising on television during hours when children might be watching.

"America's young people got a right to know about the joys of drinking hemlock," said Congressman Snavehart, "and I stand ready to defend to the death their right to know."

With growing concern about hemlock drinking, experts predicted the Snavehart Bill would face a tough fight on the floor of the House and even tougher sledding in the Senate. All forecasts were for a fascinating political struggle.

"All we ask is that the government keep its nose out of the American hemlock farmer's affairs," summed up Snavehart with passion, "and let him reap the fruits of our great free enterprise system in God-given freedom."

Meanwhile, a companion bill by Snavehart to continue the government's annual $3.7 million subsidy to hemlock growers "in order to encourage increased hemlock production" sailed through Congress on a unanimous voice vote.

A Child's First Step

Scene: The Heavenly Real Estate Office. The Landlord is seated behind his desk as his Collection Agent, Mr. Gabriel, makes his monthly report, trumpet in hand.

Gabriel (reading): And then we've experienced a 16.3 per cent increase in exploding novae in Galaxy 1673-A. The evidence points to shoddy construction.

The Landlord: All my fault, Gabriel. I'll just undertake demolition proceedings. (He waves his hand.) There. But do save the material from those 3.2 billion stars. Tomorrow, I'll build another. Anything else today?

Gabriel: No, sir. Oh, wait. There's a footnote here on that tiny little planet Earth. It's out on the fringes of Galaxy 24-137-X. Do you recall it, sir?

The Landlord: Oh, yes. I do hope the tenants are doing better.

Gabriel (a trifle smugly): Worse, sir. They're gouging up the carpet of meadows, polluting the water system, fouling the air and killing each other off at an even faster rate. You never saw such vandalism.

The Landlord (with a sigh): I so hoped they would grow up by now and meet their responsibilities.

Gabriel: Need I remind you, sir, that the first principle of sound property management is never to lease to juvenile delinquents, (raising his trumpet) Shall I sound the eviction notice?

The Landlord (wearily): I suppose so. Wait, what was that tiny flash, Gabriel?

Gabriel (with an amused smile): A crude rocket, sir.

They're planning on flying to their moon.

The Landlord (excited): Why didn't you say so? That's tremendous!

Gabriel (surprised): Tremendous? But, sir, in the vastness of the universe the distance to their moon is insignificant. A cosmic flea could reach it in half a hop.

The Landlord: But don't you see, Gabriel, it's a first step. Perhaps it means they are growing up at last.

Gabriel (smiling): Oh, far from it, sir. It may be a first step, but they are taking it for all the most childish reasons.

The Landlord: Childish? How so, Gabriel?

Gabriel: Well, you know, sir, how fond they are of their childish little clubs. Well, the American Club is going to the moon simply to show the Russian Club that it's better than they are. They're just doing it on a dare, sir.

The Landlord: The young do seek challenges, don't they?

Gabriel (frowning): Frankly, sir, they could far better use the money to fix up the place rather than gallivanting off on foolhardy adventures. And their technology really isn't ready yet for even such a minuscule flight. There's a good chance those going will all be killed.

The Landlord: The young are so brave, aren't they? And, at least, Gabriel, they will have tried.

Gabriel (lowering his trumpet): I suppose, sir, that despite all the principles of sound property management you're going to spare them once again.

The Landlord (more to himself than Gabriel): Imagine, after all these eons, they are at last about to take their first step out into my universe.

Gabriel (shaking his head): Sometimes I just don't understand you, sir.

The Landlord (with a smile): The trouble with you, Gabriel, is you've never been a father.

California, Here We Go

The Great California Earthquake was no surprise. What was odd was the immediate reaction of the rest of the country.

As word was flashed of the huge cracks opening in the Sierra Nevada mountains, Easterners and Mid-Westerners looked at each other with secretive little smiles.

"Good riddance to bad rubbish," snapped an old man in Duluth.

"It's the wrath of God on all those kooks out there," said a Christian lady in Passaic, nodding complacently.

"They had it too good too long," muttered an irritable Long Island commuter.

So the cracks widened. With a grinding roar, the mountains parted. At last, as the seers had long predicted, California was severed from the Nation.

Then, in a cataclysmic upheaval, the Nevada deserts tilted upward, the Atlantic seaboard tilted downward, and, as a Salvation Army band in Boise played, "Nearer, My God, to Thee," the rest of the United States sank slowly beneath the sea.

In Sacramento, the Governor's office acted swiftly. Within eight hours it had issued a press release entitled, "Statement of President Reagan."

"It was with extreme regret that I learned today of the loss of the rest of the United States," he said. "California has always depended on the rest of the United States for counsel in times of peace and strength in times of war.

"Nancy and I join with our people in mourning this great loss to our Nation. We always respected it. It will be missed."

In a press conference afterward, President Reagan made

it clear he was specifically excluding the U.N. enclave in New York from his statement. He also pledged "a full investigation of this further loss of Free World territory—equal to that of Mainland China or the Yalta sell-out."

But the investigation changed little. The right wing, as usual, blamed the Communists. The left wing, as usual, blamed the Pentagon. And the moderates, as usual, blamed God.

As President Reagan had predicted, California did miss the rest of the United States. But not much.

California, after all, had long produced sufficient zany clothes, far-out buildings, television dinners, concrete freeways, skull-shattering music, underground movies, bloody riots (both black and student), hippie gurus and nutty politicians to meet its needs.

Some Californians missed Las Vegas and Reno. But the conversion of Death Valley to a seaside gambling resort eased the pain.

And there were advantages, Parents no longer had to decide whether to send their offspring east to college, while sports car enthusiasts could now pick up the latest models at East Coast Port of Entry prices. And though the war in Vietnam continued, it was now a fairer fight.

But most Californians went about their hectic lives as usual. "After all," said one, referring to the loss of the country with a shrug, "we never were very much a part of it."

Foreigners generally looked on the surprising results of the long-predicted earthquake as a mixed blessing. "We'll certainly miss all those rich tourists from New York," said one Frenchman with a sigh. "But, zut alors, what a tragedy if we had lost the real Americans."

R.I.P., Liberal

Scene: The Pearly Gates. St. Peter stands, the Heavenly Roll in hand, as a weary figure trudges up the marble steps.

St. Peter: Your name, please?

Mr. Liberal: Liberal. J. Alfred Liberal (nervously). But I'm not at all sure I belong here.

St. Peter: We'll be the judge of that, Mr. Liberal. Now, if you'll recount your Good Deeds . . .

Mr. Liberal: Good Deeds? Let's see. Good Deeds. Well, when I was young, I attended Benefit Banquets. You know, for starving Armenians and things. And a lot of Charity Balls, like for crippled children . . .

St. Peter (making notes): Ate for the starving, danced for the crippled. What about the poor?

Mr. Liberal: Oh, I hardly remember a cocktail party where I didn't argue strongly for welfare legislation. And I always defended the underdog, too—the Loyalists in Spain, the Jews in Germany, the Vietnamese in Vietnam and, of course, the Neg . . . Excuse me, the Black people.

St. Peter: The Black people?

Mr. Liberal (enthusiastically): Oh, yes! The one big thing in my whole life was helping the Neg . . . Excuse me, the Blacks. Why, back in the '40s, I was the first person to have one to dinner. Ah, those were the days.

St. Peter (making a note): Drank for the poor and fed the Blacks.

Mr. Liberal (proudly): I was a life-long member of the NAACP. Then, as they advanced, I joined the Urban League and then CORE and then Friends of SNCC. But they didn't ask me to speak any more. Instead, young men in overalls would stand up and call us yellow-livered Honkies.

St. Peter: How did you retaliate?

Mr. Liberal: Oh, I applauded, of course. (Frowning) Then they threw me out. Quite rightly, too.

St. Peter: What did you join then?

Mr. Liberal (shrugging): There wasn't much left. ADA split up. The labor unions were fat. And though I opposed the war in Vietnam, I never was much for demonstrations, so the young militant groups didn't want me. In fact, my name got to be kind of a dirty word. The end came, though, in the 1968 election between Nixon and Humphrey.

St. Peter: You voted for the loser?

Mr. Liberal: Oh, I usually voted for the loser. No, it was just that I didn't have anyone to vote for.

St. Peter: What did you do then?

Mr. Liberal (simply): I died.

St. Peter: Well, let's see, you ate, danced, drank, dined and joined. Anything else?

Mr. Liberal: Yes, I felt guilty. I always felt guilty. (Guiltily) I told you I didn't belong here.

St. Peter (opening the gates): Enter, please, Mr. Liberal, and take your seat on the right of the Heavenly Throne.

Mr. Liberal (surprised): But I did so little good!

St. Peter (smiling): True. But you did so little harm.

(*From below a red glare blossoms upward amid shouts of rioters, the sirens of police and a rising crescendo of wars and revolutions.*)

St. Peter (sadly looking down): And now that your time has passed, you will be sorely missed.

4

The Generation Gap

And Let's Keep It That Way

The Greatest Generation

Once upon a time there was a man named Ben Adam, who, like most members of The Older Generation, had little hair and overwhelming guilt feelings.

He also had a son named Irwin, who, like most members of The Younger Generation, had lots of hair and an overwhelming contempt for anybody over 30.

"Man, what a mess your generation made of things," Irwin was fond of saying, several times daily. "Because of your bumbling, we face a society that's racist, militaristic, polluted, overpopulated and terrorized by the hydrogen bomb. Thanks a lot."

"I guess we're about the worst generation that ever lived," Ben Adam would say, nodding guiltily. "I'm sorry, Irwin." And Irwin would shrug and go off with his friends to smoke pot.

Ben Adam couldn't help feeling that he was in for a bit of divine wrath in return for his sins. And he was therefore somewhat shaken on awakening one night to find an Angel at the foot of his bed writing in a Golden Book.

"I have come, Ben Adam," said the Angel, "to grant you one wish."

"Me?" said Ben Adam with surprise. "Why me?"

"You have been selected by the Heavenly Computer as typical of your generation," said the Angel. "And your generation is to be rewarded for its magnificence."

"There must be some mistake," said Ben Adam with a frown. "We've been awful. We created a racist society . . ."

"Mankind has always been racist," said the Angel gently. "You were the first to admit it and attempt a remedy."

"And we militarized our democracy. Why, when I was a boy, we only had an Army of 134,000 men."

"You built an Army of four million men in hopes of bringing freedom and democracy to all the world," said the Angel. "Truly, a noble goal."

"Well, maybe," said Ben Adam. "But you can't deny that we polluted the water and the air and scattered garbage far and wide."

"That is so," said the Angel. "But the environment is polluted solely because you constructed the most affluent society the world has ever seen."

"I guess that's right," said Ben Adam. "Yet look at the Population Explosion. Famine and pestilence threaten mankind."

"Only because your generation cured diseases, increased the food supply and thereby lengthened man's life span," said the Angel. "A tremendous achievement."

"And we live in the terror of the hydrogen bomb," said Ben Adam gloomily. "What a legacy."

"Only because your generation unlocked the secrets of the atom in its search for wisdom," said the Angel. "What a glorious triumph."

"You really think so?" said Ben Adam, sitting straighter and smiling tentatively.

"Your motives were excellent, your goals ideal, your energies boundless and your achievements tremendous," said the Angel, reading from the Golden Book. "In the eons of mankind, the names of your generation, Ben Adam, lead all the rest.

And therefore, by the authority vested in me, I am empowered to grant you one wish. What shall it be?"

"I wish," said Ben Adam, the heavenly-chosen representative of The Older Generation with a sigh, "that you'd have a little talk with Irwin."

The Grave Problem Of the Tweeners

Once upon a time in the country called Wonderfuland, The Elders faced a grave problem: What to do with the Tweeners.

Now everybody in Wonderfuland had something to do—everybody but the Tweeners. The children went to school and learned mostly useful things and the grown-ups went to work and did mostly useful things. And being mostly-usefully busy, they were mostly-usefully happy.

But the Tweeners were too old to be children and too young to be grown-ups. And far too smart-alecky to have around the house.

"There's only one solution," said the eldest Elder gravely. "As soon as they're too old to be children, we must put them away in an institution until they're old enough to be grown-ups."

The other Elders recoiled in horror. "Let's think of something else," said one with a shudder. So they thought. And thought. And thought.

"Perhaps, if it were a nice institution," said a kindly Elder tentatively, "with lots of grass and trees . . ."

". . . and games for them to play," said another brightly.

". . . and cars and beer and dances," said a third enthusiastically.

". . . and if it had an impressive name," said a fourth. "I know! Let's call it College."

So the Elders built an institution, called it College and put the Tweeners away there until they could grow up.

Of course, they didn't tell them that. They told them, "You must widen your horizons, assimilate ideas and prepare for life."

To widen horizons, instill ideas and prepare them for life, The Elders staffed the College with old men called "Scholars," who weren't good for much else.

Naturally, the Scholars, being Scholars, were more interested in Scholarship than in talking to Tweeners. But twice or thrice a week they dutifully tore themselves away from their Scholarship to talk for 50 minutes about what they were interested in to the Tweeners. Like, The Sex Life of the Angiosperm. Or, The Use of the Diphthong in Etruscan Funeral Orations.

As an incentive to assimilating ideas, the Tweeners were given letters. They got big letters to wear on their sweaters for playing games well. And little tiny letters, ranging from A to F, for studying what the Scholars were interested in.

After four years, they were certified "prepared for life" and released from the institution.

Everybody was happy. The Tweeners were happy playing games, drinking beer, dancing and accumulating letters. And The Elders were happy to have them out of the house.

Then one day a Tweener looked thoughtfully around and said, "But what's all this got to do with anything?" And the other Tweeners said, somewhat surprised, that they were hanged if they knew. And pretty soon the Tweeners were demonstrating from dawn to dusk, raising a terrible fuss.

"But we've given you grass and trees and games and dances and beer and letters," said the Elders, rather plaintively.

"What is it you want?"

"Frankly, we're darned if we know," admitted a Tweener Leader, scratching his head. "But whatever it is, this isn't it."

Moral: College is a wonderful institution—for those who want to grow up in an institution.

Unity Through Pollution

Once upon a time a young man named Irwin gave up protests. He gave up protesting Vietnam, the draft, sexually segregated rest rooms and pigs on campus.

"Ecology is the one true cause!" said Irwin nobly, just like most young people of the time. "I shall devote myself to making a more beautiful world."

"Oh, my beamish boy," cried his happy mother, like mothers everywhere. "I knew you'd give up those silly demonstrations and settle down to doing good."

"Everybody's for ecology, son," said his proud father, like fathers everywhere. "At least we've found a common cause that will close the generation gap."

And it did. Irwin joined the Students for Delightful Surroundings. He spent his days spearing litter with a pointy stick. And his evenings circulating petitions.

The older generation finally approved of the younger generation. Everybody was happy.

But after a year or so, Irwin and his young friends discovered that spearing litter seemed somewhat joyless. And circulating petitions seemed somewhat pointless. Nothing much got done.

Oh, Congress passed a few bills. The corporations talked about "corporate responsibility." The President said the local communities must do more. The local communities said Washington must do more.

So the air got smoggier, the waters fouler, the litter deeper and the supermarkets more crowded.

"These things take time, son," said Irwin's father nervously. "At least you're doing good, dear," said Irwin's mother uneasily.

At 5:14 p.m. the following Tuesday, the SDS staged a lie-in on the Pasadena Freeway. The resultant traffic jam, extending from Anaheim to Azusa, eventually had to be paved over.

The Nation was outraged. Editorial writers thundered: "No little band of radicals, no matter how just their cause, has the right to . . ."

The next day, the SDS blew up 16 dams to create wild rivers, toppled 42 oil derricks to promote clean beaches and booed every passing baby carriage in Central Park.

The following week, they dynamited every sewer in Decatur, N.J., sabotaged the No Deposit Bottle Factory in Billings, S.C. and tried to burn down the heart of Los Angeles—but they couldn't find it.

Young Irwin, home on the lam, was confronted by his tearful mother. "Why don't you quit that radical SDS, dear," she pleaded, "and join the nice, respectable Sierra Club instead?"

"Those Uncle Smokeys!" snorted Irwin. "They just want to conserve the wilderness we've got. But we're going to make the whole country into one big wilderness!"

"But, son," pleaded his father, "think of the innocent people you're hurting in this cause of yours."

"The great thing about ecology as a cause," said Irwin happily, "is that everybody's guilty."

And with that he proceeded to set fire to the family car, tip over the family barbecue and smash up all two-and-a-half toilets in the family's two-and-a-half-bath house.

When he'd gone, his parents ruefully surveyed the wreckage. "I think I liked it better," said his mother with a sigh, "when he was only mad at the President, the university, the police and the Army."

Moral: The generation gap won't be closed until those exuberant young fools grow old. Or we old fools grow exuberant.

Sir Walter Raleigh's Historic Mistake

Many attempts have been made to rewrite history. The best, undoubtedly, is that well-known work, "A Better History of the World." An excerpt follows.

It was in 1585 while on an expedition to Virginia that Sir Walter Raleigh got drunk, took a wrong turn and missed keeping an appointment with the Tabac Indian chiefs. Instead, he found himself in the happy village of the Merriwanna Tribe.

Not knowing one Indian from another, Sir Walter innocently accepted a peace pipe, politely took half a dozen deep drags and pronounced these historic words:

"Man, this is the real stuff!"

The introduction of merriwanna, as it became known, into the civilized world changed the entire course of history. In fact, nothing of historical interest happened for the next 300 years.

An illustration of this dearth was the Thirty Seconds War. The conflict lasted as long as it took for the two armies to line up and view each other's glittering array of finely honed halberts and swords. At that moment a private in the rear ranks cried, "Hey, you cats, let's cool it." And everybody went home.

For the trouble with merriwanna was that instead of instilling courage, like alcohol, it instilled euphoria. Nor did it produce fits of depression or morning-after retribution.

Thus it quickly replaced alcohol as a means of escape. And while some abused it, as they had alcohol, most were content to go about their daily lives and relax with a couple of pipesful in the evening.

The cumulative effect was to soothe the frayed nerves of society. And it was most difficult to drum up much enthusiasm for marching off to kill somebody.

So nothing much happened historically until 1912 when an enterprising agricultural scientist rediscovered the tabac weed.

He found that "tabacco," as he named it, produced a much bigger, broader leaf than merriwanna and could thus be dried, shredded and rolled into cigarettes far more economically. "I'll make a million," he said rubbing his hands.

Unfortunately, he was quickly hauled up before the Pure Food & Drug Administration, which demanded to know what this tabacco did for you.

"Well, first of all," said the scientist proudly, "it gives you lung cancer."

He was branded a dangerous charlatan and a rational Government immediately made the sale, transportation or possession of tabacco a felony.

While tabacco is still smoked clandestinely by jazz musicians, hippies and thrill-seeking youth, every study shows that its illegal use can lead to experiments with heroin, LSD, speed and other equally dangerous drugs.

Indeed, one of the gravest worries of most fathers today is that their children will somehow get hooked on tabacco and end up emphysema-ridden, nicotine-stained addicts—slaves to a 30-joint-a-day habit.

Probably all that saves a father's sanity when he envisions such a fate for his offspring is to light up a soothing, euphoric pipeful of merriwanna.

"If these kids today have to smoke," he'll say, shaking his head, "why can't they smoke something that's good for them?"

The True Christian

Once upon a time there was a young man named Irwin who devoted his waking hours to Gestalt jogging, transcendental massage, elementary Zoroastrianism, advanced astrology and mastering the Double Lotus position.

Naturally, his parents didn't understand him.

"Irwin," his father would say wearily, "I know there's a generation gap. But all these weird religions! Why can't you be more like your mother and me? What's wrong with Christianity?"

"I guess it's that I never tried it, Dad," said Irwin. And being a dutiful son at heart he actually went down to The Billy Graham Crusade the next time it hit town. He came home a drastically changed young man.

"I've heard the call, Dad," he said, his eyes shining. "I've become a true Christian."

"That's great, son," said his father, clapping him on the back. "At last we see eye to eye on things."

"Right, Dad. And you'll be proud to know I've joined The Juniors for Jesus."

"The what?" said his father nervously.

"It's a Christian-action group, Dad," said Irwin, bubbling with the enthusiasm of the young. "Our goal is to see that our loved ones lead true Christian lives so that we may all enter the Kingdom of Heaven together. Now how much did you give to the poor last year?"

"The poor?" said his father uneasily. "Well, we gave $50 to the United Crusade."

Irwin shook his head. "Look, Dad, we've got money in

the bank and more food than we can eat, while poor people are going hungry. Remember what the Bible says about a rich man's chances of entering heaven."

So, to encourage Irwin in his new-found faith, his parents agreed to give half their savings and ten per cent of their income to charity. It meant they had to give up their trip to Europe. And Irwin's father did miss his golf club, but it seemed worthwhile.

The next week Irwin's father came home to find his new $35 slacks missing. "Irwin gave them to a magazine solicitor," explained his wife. "The poor man did look a bit threadbare."

Gradually, the family's wardrobe diminished garment by garment. "Actually," explained Irwin happily, "a true Christian needs only enough to keep himself warm."

And then half the furniture vanished. "What is a man profited if he shall have two sofas, three end tables and 16 chairs," said Irwin, "and lose his own soul?"

They lost the family car after an accident in which Irwin's father was painfully injured in the left hip. The other party, though clearly in the wrong, sued. The suit went uncontested. For as Irwin pointed out, it was his father's Christian duty to "turn the other cheek."

Fortunately, just as his parents were reaching wit's end, Irwin picked up a copy of the I Ching, became converted to Ecumenical Taoism and went off to Kathmandu to chew betel nuts and see how long he could grow his toenails.

His parents heaved a collective sigh of relief. "Of course, it was your fault," his mother told his father, "telling him he ought to be a Christian."

"I meant," said his father defensively, "a Christian like us."

Moral: Don't worry about today's generation gap. It could be worse.

Strange Sex Rites Of the Ugulaps—V

Herewith is Chapter V from that much-read anthropological study, "Strange Sex Practices Among the Ugulap Savages."

This chapter, unfortunately, deals not with sex practices, but with the natives' disgraceful custom of smoking Ghrass.

Indigenous to the Ugulap soil is a hardy plant known to the savages as "Ghrass." They cultivate it carefully for its leaves which they dry and shred. The dried leaves are then placed in a clay pipe, called a "roech," lit, and passed from hand to hand.

The ritual is unvarying. As each native inhales the sweet, acrid smoke, he rolls his eyes and repeats the phrase: "Man, this is the real stuff!"

The smoking of Ghrass appears to induce a mild euphoric effect. While some natives abuse it, most seem content with a relaxing pipeful before the evening meal, although many overindulge on festive occasions known as "Pott-Partees" (probably from the French, "pot-pouri").

Unlike most backward tribes, the use of alcohol is unknown among the Ugulaps.

Legend has it that a native named "Mar-Tee-Nee" discovered the secret of fermenting juniper berries. He invited his friends to drink of the juices and they caroused long into the night, singing and fighting and extolling the discovery of Mar-Tee-Nee.

In the morning, however, each was visited by the wrath of the Gods, according to the legend. Mar-Tee-Nee was banished and the chiefs decreed that anyone fermenting juniper berries would have his head squeezed in a vise as fitting retribution.

Attempts have been made, of course, to stamp out the disgraceful Ghrass cult. One of which we have a complete record is that of The Reverend G. Grisgrombe Grommet, who visited the Ugulaps in his sloop, "Rosinante," only last year. In his report home to his Board of Missions, the Reverend wrote:

"Initially, I attempted to persuade the natives to renounce Ghrass through the use of logic. I pointed out to them, quite accurately, that smoking this foul weed clearly made them happy. And that therefore it was obviously sinful. But they seem to have no concept of sin.

"It occurred to me that introducing a civilized substitute might be the answer. Fortunately, I had a carton of American cigarettes and a few magazines aboard.

"The natives were fascinated by the cigarettes and lit them at once. After inhaling deeply and coughing considerably, each waited with an expectant look on his face. Finally, the Chief asked, 'What do these do for you?'

" 'Absolutely nothing,' I reassured him. I then showed the natives advertisements in the magazines depicting beautiful men and women smoking cigarettes, hoping these child-like people would think cigarettes would make them beautiful, too.

"Unfortunately, one of the young natives who could decipher English, stumbled on a public service message written by the American Cancer Society and read it aloud to his brethren.

" 'Now we know what these do for you,' said the Chief.

Some natives argued for flailing me alive. But others contended I was obviously a 'koo-koo-head,' a phrase apparently meaning one who is protected from punishment—which at least shows their respect for us men of the cloth.

"In any event, I made my escape. In closing, I must say I see little hope that these backward savages will ever renounce their primitive Ghrass Cult and accept the blessings of civilization."

The Great Adult Counter-Revolution

It was on September 23, 1972, that a mob of angry adults, shouting "Punks off campus!" stormed through the gates of Skarewe University and smashed every window in the Student Union.

"This is the dawn of the counter-revolution!" cried their leader, Sidney Snell, a 43-year-old bank teller. "We are going to tear down this nihilist, violence-prone student society and build a better, more humane one in its place."

Snell explained to the television cameras that he represented APS—the Adults for a Polite Society. And he promised further militant action, "Violence and rudeness is all these kids understand," he said.

The students were shocked. SDS leader Abbie Hayden called a mass protest rally the next day. His remarks, however, were drowned out by a claque of APS faculty members, chanting, "Punk! Punk! Punk!"

University President Grandville Grommet, himself, poured a sack of fresh manure over young Hayden's head. Humanities Professor Hadley R. Hadley, something of a hothead, completed the disruption of the meeting by setting fire to the rostrum.

News coverage of the two events was devoured eagerly in millions of American homes. It fanned a long-smoldering spark. Middle-aged eyes lit up. Over-40 shoulders squared. And more than one father told his son to go get a haircut or he'd hit him with a two-by-four.

Across the land, APS chapters sprang up. Militant middle-agers met in cells beneath the portraits of Spiro Agnew and Ronald Reagan to operate clandestine mimeograph machines calling all adults to the counter-revolution.

"Never Trust Anybody Under 30!," "Off the Punks!," "Up the Bloodbath!" and "Who's Running Things Around Here Anyway?" became universal rallying cries.

Allowances were canceled, cars reclaimed and strict curfews applied in millions of homes. A group of over-40 fanatics known as The Hourmen were blamed for a series of bombings of student hangouts and rock and roll stations.

Student leaders, wary and apprehensive, demanded police protection. But there was no question whose side the police were on.

The high point came when Snell of the APS met young Hayden of the SDS on the nationally televised program, "Jaw to Jaw."

"How do you expect to reform our student society," demanded Hayden angrily, "through rudeness and violence?"

"In exactly the same way," replied Snell smugly, as the middle-aged audience cheered, "that you expected to reform ours."

Outnumbered, outgunned and out of money, the students finally were forced to surrender. Laws were passed raising the voting age to 30, requiring everyone under 21 to address everyone over 21 as "Sir," and combining the universities with the penal system.

"Now that the counter-revolution has at last succeeded," said Snell triumphantly, "our young people will grow up to be just as tolerant, just as humane and just as non-violent as we are."

And, by George, they did!

The Son of Horatio Alger

Once upon a time there was a young man named Horatio Alger who lived in a country suffering under a Great Depression.

Times were terrible. Horatio couldn't find a job. He had to share a run-down flat with ten other unemployed bums. They wore odd, cast-off clothes. They had no soap, no razor blades, no privacy and not much hope.

And all they had to eat were beans, bagels and boiled rutabagas—day after day.

"But I shall persevere!" said Horatio grimly. "I shall persevere so that my son will have a better life. He will have a decent home, decent clothes, decent food and a decent job. He shall never have to live like this."

And Horatio persevered.

He found a job lifting bags and toting bales for 20 cents an hour, 12 hours a day. He suffered. He persevered.

He formed a union. He called a strike. The police clubbed him on the head. The Establishment scorned him as "an anarchist" and "a troublemaker." He suffered. But he persevered.

"I must do my part to reform society and make this a better world," he said. And he did.

Thanks in part to his efforts, times changed. Minimum wages, old age pensions, unemployment insurance and the eight-hour day came into being. Prosperity gradually returned.

At last Horatio's suffering and perseverance were rewarded. Like most of his generation he now had a decent home, decent clothes, decent food, a decent job, two cars in the garage and chicken every Sunday.

And he had a son, Horatio Junior.

"It was all worth it," said Horatio proudly and happily as he watched the lad grow up, "to know that he will never have to undergo what I underwent."

Junior, as sons inevitably will, grew up. "What, Dad," he asked one day, "should I make the goal of my life?"

"Why, son," replied Horatio with some surprise, "the goal of life, of course, is to get a decent job so that you can have a decent home, decent clothes, decent food, two cars in the garage and chicken every Sunday."

"But I've already got all that," said Junior. And a week later he dropped out.

Junior joined a commune and lived in a run-down flat with ten other unemployed bums. They wore odd, cast-off clothes. They had no soap, razor blades or privacy and, in conformity with their Zoroastrian religion, they ate nothing but beans, bagels and boiled rutabagas—day after day.

The police clubbed them on the head. The Establishment scorned them as "anarchists" and "trouble-makers." But Junior persevered.

"I must do my part," he said, "to reform society and make this a better world."

"But why, son?" cried Horatio, wringing his hands. "Why?"

"The trouble with you, Dad," said his son sadly, "is that you don't understand the finer things in life."

Moral: Cheer up. Our grandchildren will be just like us.

The Hippie Who Became a Square

Once upon a time there was a young man named Irving who was a hippie.

He wasn't a good hippie who loved and created and rejoiced. He could have done many wonderful hippie things—like dancing in the mountain meadows or making seashell necklaces or learning to play the flute.

But, unfortunately, he was a bad hippie—the kind who smoked pot, drank wine and sat around all day muttering, "What a dumb world it is. Life is sure a drag."

His parents, Mr. and Mrs. Wilbur Wasp, were very ashamed of him. "Why don't you cut your hair, buy some decent clothes, get a job and make something of yourself," they told him—about 27 times a day.

It seemed as though Irving would never change. But one evening he got stoned in front of the television set and inadvertently sat through three old Doris Day movies in a row.

Something inside Irving snapped. In the morning he woke up a square.

He cut his hair, bought a $49.95 suit and got a job. His parents were very proud of him. "At last," Mr. and Mrs. Wasp told all their friends, "Irving has found himself."

Irving's job was to make cardboard cartons to contain fancy gift packages which contained handsomely-shaped bottles which contained cheap whisky.

He found his job very interesting—for about the first 15 minutes. But he soon discovered he could fold the cartons without thinking, without thinking of anything at all.

He did this eight hours a day. Monday through Friday.

But he had job security. He had a medical plan, a dental plan and a retirement plan, for which he'd be eligible in 38 years and 11 months.

Naturally, he didn't smoke pot any more. He smoked filter-tipped, mentholated, king-sized cigarettes instead. They often gave him a sore throat and a cough.

Naturally, he didn't drink cheap wine any more. He drank bourbon and 7-Up instead. It often made him nauseous at night and hung-over in the morning.

Now Irving could have done many wonderful square things—like bicycle riding in the park, making cloisonne coffee tables or learning to play the piano. But he preferred watching television instead.

He would come home from work, heat a tee-vee dinner and sit in front of his set from the "I Love Lucy" re-run right through the Johnny Carson Show. He could even tell you what was on every station at any hour without looking at the paper.

Occasionally his parents would visit him. "How are things going, Irving?" they would say:

"What a dumb world it is," Irving would mutter. "Life is sure a drag."

Nothing shocked Mr. and Mrs. Wasp more. "How can you say that, Irving," they would ask, "when you look so neat, dress so well and have such a good job?

"Son," they would say, embracing him, "you don't know how proud you've made us."

Moral: If you're bound and determined to lead a dumb life, be a square. At least you'll make your parents happy.

The Kids' Lib

Heaven knows, Margaret and I tried to be good parents to Irving. We read him all the Dr. Seuss books, encouraged him to watch Sesame Street, never bought him war toys and always reasoned with him instead of punishing him.

To teach him the value of money as he grew older, we gave him $2 a week allowance in return for two hours of chores around the house. And we paid him 50 cents an hour for babysitting his little brother.

It was this last, I suppose, that sparked the crisis. In some fashion, he discovered that while he was away at the Blueberry Hill Happiness Camp last summer, we paid Mrs. Grommet down the block $1.75 an hour for precisely the same task.

How well I recall the militant look on little Irving's 12-year-old face as he marched up to me at the breakfast table the following morning.

"Father," he said grimly, "you are an adult chauvinist pig!"

My initial reaction was one of shock. "How can you say that, Irving?" I gasped.

"Equal pay for equal work," said Irving. "That goes for babysitting. Further, that $1 an hour you give me for chores violates the Federal Minimum Wage Law."

"But you're not engaged in interstate commerce, Irving," I protested.

"It's the morality that matters," Irving said. "For thousands of years you adultists have been exploiting us children because we're weak and unorganized. You love us only for our hard-working little bodies. You have brainwashed us into believing we are inferior creatures, fit only to serve your every whim."

"But haven't I been good to you, Irving?" I asked.

"Benevolent paternalism!" snapped Irving. "Childhood freedom now!"

Thus were the seeds of The Children's Liberation Front sown.

We all know how it spread across the land. The publication of 13-year-old Betsy Freeman's book, "The Childhood Mystique," the restaurant picketing protesting inferior "child's portions," the lunch counter sit-ins demanding lower counters and shorter stools, and the constant marches for an end to discriminatory drinking, smoking, voting and driving laws—not to mention G-rated movies.

At last, the most oppressed minority in the Nation was aroused in righteous wrath. At last, the truly little people were speaking out. At last, I blew my stack.

It was the day Irving came home from a Kids' Lib rally and demanded the keys to the family car, a separate checking account and room service on the grounds that, as he put it, "Youth must be served!"

Something inside me snapped. "If you want to wear the pants around here, Irving," I said, "you need a belt." So I belted him.

He's been meek as a churchmouse ever since. Margaret looks at me with new respect. Life seems fuller and richer somehow.

Call me an adultist chauvinist pig. Call me an exploiter, an oppressor. But let us all treasure our little children. Remember, fellow adults, they are the last oppressible minority we've got.

The Strange Cult of Security Worship

Once upon a time, the country called Wonderfuland fell on hard times. There wasn't enough food or enough warm clothes or enough jobs or enough of anything to go around.

Many people worried where their next meal was coming from. Parents worried how to feed their children and keep them warm. Riots and strikes and demagogues shattered the night. Everybody was terribly, terribly insecure.

So they raised one god above all the others, the god called Security.

Now men had worshipped Security ever since time began, but none more devoutly than the people of Wonderfuland. They devoted their whole lives to seeking the blessings of Security.

From morning to night they labored for Security. In strange rituals, they dug gold from the ground and buried it in the ground for Security. They built awesome weapons to protect their Security. And they sacrificed their sons in strange little wars in strange little places—all in the name of Security.

And Security, pleased by their devotions, showered blessings upon them until Wonderfuland became the richest, mightiest nation the world had ever known.

So at long last, for the first time in history, there was enough food and enough warm clothes and enough jobs and enough everything to go around.

"At last we have the blessings of Security," said the people happily. And, not knowing what else to do, they went right on laboring for Security.

Pretty soon, they had more than enough food, more than

enough clothes, more than enough gold and weapons so awesome they could never use them.

Each man, to show his devotion, strove to accumulate the symbols of Security—a bigger car, a bigger house and scrolls of paper attesting to his faith, scrolls known, naturally enough, as "securities."

Then a strange thing happened. The more blessings of Security the people of Wonderfuland enjoyed, the more they worried about losing them.

They worried that their cars would be dented or their houses burned down or their securities rendered worthless. They worried that the gold they could never use would somehow drain away. They worried that the weapons they could never use would somehow destroy them. And they worried vaguely whether sacrificing their sons in holy wars for Security was the right thing to do.

Sometimes, in the middle of the night, they would awake to wonder what life was all about. But they seldom talked about that. And they drank their martinis dry.

Meanwhile, their children grew and it came time to give them a goal to seek. The parents gave them the only goal they knew:

"You must," said the parents devoutly, "get good grades so you can get in a good college so you can get a good job so you can make good money so you can enjoy the eternal blessings of Security."

But the children, who had never known hunger or want, looked at their parents uneasily. And they put on strange clothes and took strange drugs and danced off to strange music to seek strange gods they might never find.

So it came to pass that everybody in Wonderfuland was terribly, terribly insecure—the young because they had no god to worship and the old because they did.

Moral: Security's a fine goal—until you've got it.

A Cause for Celebration

I sat slouched in my chair in front of the television set, gazing awestruck with the astronauts through the window of Apollo XII as the craters of a golden moon sailed overhead.

And I felt with them the excitement, the strangeness and the fearful thrill of it all. What a great adventure for these brave men! And for me.

For voyaging to the moon has been the high adventure of my generation, we instinctive members of The Silent Majority. What a triumph our leap toward the stars has been—the astronauts in their spaceship, the rest of us in our armchairs.

When the commercial came on, I went to the kitchen for a glass of milk, still excited. On the table was a button a schoolgirl had sent me. Its message was the cry of so many of the new generation. It read simply:

"Celebrate life!"

As I often have these past days, I thought of the peace march the week before. All those thousands upon thousands of young people waving placards and singing and laughing and smiling at each other with that joyous rapport of those who have come together in what they feel is a worthy cause.

And once again it seemed to me that most of them were not so much protesting the war as they were, quite literally, celebrating life.

My generation was in the minority. For we instinctive members of The Silent Majority are reluctant to demonstrate in public, to draw attention to ourselves, to become vulnerable. Yet we who were there felt for the moment, I think, what the young people felt.

What was most vivid to me was not the long march nor the dreary succession of angry speakers, but two young girls dancing barefoot in the grass. We picknicked and watched, we older people, as they leaped and pirouetted and dipped, their long hair flying, their bare legs flashing, their eyes half closed as they became one with the music and the day. How fully they were celebrating life.

What a lovely phrase that is—"Celebrate life!" How deeply wise. For surely the first secret of life is to live it—to live it as fully as one can. But, ah, to celebrate it!

To me it connotes a reverence for the sacredness of life, a gratitude for this most precious of all gifts. What greater cause for a daily celebration. And if we all celebrated, who could kill or oppress or hate his living fellow man?

How incredible it is that the young, who are so wrong in so many things, could be so right.

Thinking of all this, I returned to the television set, but the illusion that I was part of the high adventure was gone. I now saw the sides of the box and the knobs. It was now but a machine for stimulating the emotions of the sedentary—of us who watch rather than do.

How tragic it is that we have a Silent Majority. How tragic they're silent; how tragic they're a majority. I saw them sitting in these exciting times silently watching life in a box as the young celebrants danced joyously by. It's no wonder they hate them so.

I swore then that I too, would celebrate life. But my shell has grown hard and my nest is warm and soft. And as I watched the golden image of a pock-marked moon on the little plate of glass, I knew the saddest truth of all:

My generation may reach for the stars from its armchairs, but we will never dance barefoot on the grass.

5

All Men Are Brothers

And They Fight Like It

Take a City to Lunch

"We're making real progress," said my friend, George Washington X. "Nobody calls me 'Colored' any more.

"I attribute this to the National Association for the Advancement of Colored People which got folks to stop calling me a 'Colored People' and start calling me a 'Negro.'

"There was a real advance. But then the Student Non-Violent Co-ordinating Committee got violent about Black Power and people began calling me 'Black.'

"I figured this was about as far as one man could struggle upward in one lifetime. But, much to my surprise, they've now come up with a brand new name for me."

What's that?

"Now they call me," said Mr. X with pardonable pride, "a 'City,' "

A "City"? "That's right," said Mr. X. "You just listen to our leaders—Nixon, Humphrey, Spiro T. Whatshisname. Every one of them is going around saying, 'We must do something about the growing crisis of our Cities.'

"That's me they're talking about, man. And that's not the half of it. More often than not, they get specific and call me an 'Urban Core,' 'A Decaying Innercity' and an 'Impacted Area.'

"Now, I don't much mind being an Urban Core. I guess a man could stand an Urban Core moving in next door to him. But would you want your sister to marry an Impacted Area?

"Naturally, they got other names for me down South. To George Wallace I'm either a 'Bearded Pseudo-Intellectual,' which I kind of like, or, best of all, a 'Power-Mad Federal Bureaucracy.'

"How about that? Only in America could a little Colored boy aspire to grow up to be the whole Federal Government."

He must be terribly proud of an achievement like that.

"You bet," said Mr. X. "And it fills my heart to hear how every politician wants to do something for me. Either they want to revitalize us Urban Cores or make us Decaying Innercities thrive again.

"At first, I figured I was going to get free vitamin pills. But it turns out they merely aim to kick me out of my house and cut off the welfare check."

That didn't sound too promising.

"Well," said Mr. X philosophically, "it sure beats Reestablishing Law & Order in Our Strife-torn Cities."

He was against Law & Order?

"Do you expect me," he said with surprise, "to be in favor of shooting us uppity Niggers?"

I thanked Mr. X for providing a clearer understanding of what on earth the candidates will be constantly talking about in the upcoming campaign. But I couldn't see where it would contribute much to Mr. X's progress toward full equality.

"Maybe not," he agreed. "But I sure am building one hell of a vocabulary."

Colonel Stonewall, Visionary

The House Un-American Activities Committee plans to investigate the Black militant movement to see if it gets its funds from "a foreign power." Actually, such suspicions are groundless.

The largest single contributor to the Black militants, according to documented records, is a patriotic American with a life-long interest in race relations—Colonel Jefferson Lee Stonewall of Mudge, Mississippi.

In addition to his generous financial help, Colonel Stonewall also provides expert counseling, guidance and long-range planning to the movement.

It was the Colonel, of course, who first conceived the current demands for separate Black Studies Programs in the universities with Black students, Black faculties and Black administrators.

"Separate but equal, that's our motto," said the Colonel, happily fanning himself with his Panama. "Why, I'm even teaching my Black friends some old college yells to drum up the proper spirit. Like:

"Two-four-six-eight, we don't wanna integrate!"

Charges that the lack of qualified Black professors and administrators would make such Black colleges anything but equal are dismissed by Colonel Stonewall with an airy wave of his cigar.

"They'll be equal to each other, son," he said. "And they'll go a long way toward preserving the cherished Black way of life."

This, of course, is one of Colonel Stonewall's long-range

goals for the movement. He is believed to have played a major role in developing the Black militants' stand against racial mixing.

Slogans he contributed include, "Defend Black womanhood," "Preserve the purity of the Black race" and "Would you want your sister to marry a Honkie?"

The Colonel sees the establishment of separate but equal Black colleges as only the first step toward achieving these ambitious ends.

"We're already planning a massive bus strike in Montgomery, Alabama," he said, "to demand that the last five rows in every bus be reserved for Blacks.

A true visionary, the Colonel foresees the day when no self-respecting Black man would think of living in a Honkie neighborhood.

The Army will have all-Black units, he says. Theater balconies will be roped off for Blacks only. And Blacks will have their own hotels, restaurants and bus depot waiting rooms.

"But the dignity of the Black man," he tells his enthusiastic Black militant friends, "will never be assured until he has his very own drinking fountains throughout the land—clearly labeled for his exclusive use.

"I only hope," he says with the sigh of an idealist ahead of his times, "that I live to see the day."

The acceptance of a White Southerner like Colonel Stonewall by the Black militant leaders has come as a surprise to many observers. But not to the Colonel.

"Why, it's plain as day they recognize me for what I am," he said, complacently flicking his cigar. "A soul brother."

Little Black Tombo Becomes a Man

Once upon a time there was a little black boy named Tombo. He was a slave.

"All I want in life," he said, "is to be free, to be equal and to be a man."

Then one day—Hallelujah!—his white masters freed him. "Now that you are free," they said, "you must work hard to become equal to us."

Little Black Tombo nodded. "Yes," he said, "now that I'm free, I must become equal to you so that I, too, can be a man. How do I become equal?"

"The problem," said some Nice White People, "is an educational one. You must get an education. Then you will be equal to us."

So some Nice White People gave him an education. It wasn't easy. It took years and years and years. But at last Little Black Tombo had an education.

"It's funny," said Tom (for, being educated, he had changed his name), "but I still don't feel equal to you."

"The problem," said some Nice White People, "is an economic one. You must have a good job. Then you will be equal to us."

So some Nice White People gave Tom a job. It wasn't easy. It took years and years and years. But at last Tom had a job.

"It's funny," said Tom, "but I still don't feel equal to you."

"The problem," said some Nice White People, "is an environmental one. You must move out of the ghetto into a nice house like ours. Then you will be equal to us."

So some Nice White People got him a house. It wasn't easy. They had to pass laws saying other white people had to sell him a house whether they liked it or not. But at last Tom got a nice house.

"It's funny," said Tom, "but I still don't feel equal to you."

"The problem," said some Nice White People, "is sociological. You must dress like us, talk like us and think like us. Then, obviously, you will be equal to us."

So some Nice White People taught him how to dress and talk and think and they even invited him to their cocktail parties.

The hostess would squeeze his hand warmly (though she never kissed him on the cheek). And the men would clap him on the back and ask him his opinion (but only about racial matters).

This time, Tom didn't say much at all. He grew a beard, put on dark glasses, changed his name to Tombo X and shouting, "Black is beautiful," hit the first two Nice White People he saw over the head.

They were, of course, deeply hurt. "After all we've done for you," they said. "Don't you realize you're throwing away everything we struggled together for? Now you'll never feel equal to us."

"It's funny," said Tombo X, smiling, "but at last I feel like a man."

Moral: You can think a black man is free and equal. But first you must think of him, not as a black, but as a man.

The Black Man's Burden

It was a grim scene—the day the militant Black leader, Stokely Rapp, came home early from a demonstration and caught his son, Tad, lounging on the corner with two White boys.

"March into the house, I want to talk with you," Rapp told his son sternly. Then forcing a smile, he said to the other two, "I think maybe you boys better be running along home."

Once in the kitchen, Rapp wasted no time. "What did I tell you about playing with Honkies?" he demanded.

Tad made a circle on the floor with the toe of his shoe. "You used to let me play with them in the park," he said with a touch of defiance.

"That was when you were small," said Rapp. "I played with them when I was small, too. Why, I was practically raised by a Honkie woman. But you're almost a man now. You're going to have to take a position of responsibility in the Black community. You want people going around saying you're a Honkie lover?"

"Well, no, I guess not," said Tad. "But I don't see what's so wrong with them. Some of my best friends are Honkies."

Rapp shook his head. "You'd betray all I've fought for all my life, just like that," he said sadly. "Do you know why we kicked them out of The Movement? Because you can't trust them. I never met a Honkie I'd trust an inch."

"But why, Dad?"

"It's something in their blood. They're greedy for power. They're clannish. You let one in, you've got to let them all in. And first you know, they'll take over. Anthropologists will tell you they're different."

"But some of them seem just like us."

"Sure, you'll meet a few who try to pass for Black. They learn our music, our way of talking. But I can spot them every time. They don't have any natural sense of rhythm."

"But if we don't learn to live with them, Dad . . ."

"Live with them? What's beautiful, Tad?"

"Black is beautiful."

"And conversely, White is ugly. Just ask yourself, son, do you want a skinny-lipped, pointy-nosed Honkie to marry your sister?"

"I guess not, Dad. But I can't help feeling sorry for them."

"And rightly, son. They're burdened with 400 years of guilt and neuroses. But we can't be expected to wipe that out overnight. Gradualism is the only answer. And meantime, son, our one duty is to defend Black womanhood, uphold the sacred concept of Black Power and preserve the purity of our race."

"I guess I understand, Dad. And I'm sorry. But what makes Honkies that way?"

"Guilt, son. They're guilty of the one crime that above all others destroys the human soul."

"What's that, Dad?"

"Racism," said Rapp, slapping his palm on the kitchen table. "Never forget, son, that every Honkie you meet is, at heart, a bigot."

Beatrice Pearson, In Memoriam

Beatrice Moss Pearson died last week after a long illness. She was very old and very tired and very black.

She had been cleaning white people's houses for more than half a century.

She was . . . I started to say that she was "our cleaning lady," the way white people do. But she wasn't ours. What an offense against God that phrase is.

She used to come to our house once a week before she grew too old and tired to work any more.

I suppose she was what some white people call "the good old-fashioned colored type." You know, "a real jewel," "one of the family," "the kind you can hardly find any more."

I suppose she was. She was a big woman in a spotless, starched white dress. She ironed beautifully, scrubbed diligently and cooked marvelously.

But, after all, she had been ironing and scrubbing and cooking for white people for more than half a century.

I don't know precisely how old she was. Neither did she. I tried to check for her once when she applied for Social Security. But they didn't keep records on the birth of black children in her part of Texas when she was born.

It must have been about the turn of the century. For she remembered seeing Halley's Comet in 1910 as a young girl. And her daddy beat her for staying out late to watch its flaming passage across the night sky.

I can still visualize her, a slim young girl standing on a hillside, head tilted back, awed by the wonder and promise of the universe.

When she was 13 she started cleaning white people's houses. She had neither the education nor the opportunity to do anything else. She never did.

Yes, she was "the kind you can hardly find any more." She was honest and cheerful and hard-working. But she was more than that. She was gentle and intelligent and loving and funny.

She was also deeply religious. When she had a major operation a few years back, she saw God on the wall of her hospital room. But she never talked about it much. Not to us.

After that, she couldn't work any more. We used to visit her in her house across town. "A nice house in a nice neighborhood" was her one extravagance. It was a nice little stucco house on a nice little hillside. She listened to the baseball games on the radio and watched television and she was happy when her granddaughter lived with her for a while.

She had raised her four children as best she could, but each had rebelled in one way or another. I don't think she ever quite understood why.

None of her children will spend their lives cleaning white people's houses. I am glad of that. No, you can hardly find her kind any more.

We went to see her in the hospital the night before she died. She didn't know us. Death was almost on her and death is ugly and my wife cried.

As she lay on the rumpled bed murmuring strange dreams, I took her hand and kissed it. I don't know why. Her skin was surprisingly soft, like a young girl's. It seemed the saddest thing of all.

Yet grief passes and only anger is left. I am angered, not by her death, but by her life. "Life," President Kennedy once said, "is unfair."

So damnably unfair.

Man's Black Magic

Scene: The Heavenly Real Estate Office. The Landlord, thoughtfully stroking his long white beard, is listening to the annual year-end report from his collection agent, Mr. Gabriel.

Gabriel: . . . and the exploding novae in Sector 4782 now seem under control, but that runaway galaxy in the 534th Quadrant still requires your attention, sir.

Landlord (wearily): It isn't easy keeping a billion trillion stars in their courses. Is that all, Gabriel?

Gabriel: No, sir. I still have the special report on that tiny planet you love so.

The Landlord (pleased): Ah, yes, Earth, my little blue-green jewel. (frowning) Are the tenants still gouging up my mountain meadows, burning holes in my forested carpets and befouling my blue seas and crystalline air?

Gabriel: Yes, sir. And they're still brawling, fighting and killing each other off. (hopefully raising his trumpet) Shall I sound the eviction notice now, sir?

The Landlord: Wait, Gabriel. There is one thing I don't understand. Don't they know they are all children of God?

Gabriel: Yes, sir, they all know that.

The Landlord: Then how can a child of God bring himself to maim or kill another child of God?

Gabriel: Oh, he doesn't sir. First he performs a magic rite changing his enemy into something less than human. Then, when his enemy is no longer a child of God, he maims or kills him in good conscience.

The Landlord: What an awesome power! How do they manage this incredibly complex transformation?

Gabriel: Very simply. Look down there, sir. Can you see through that blanket of smog? Now take those two fine men in blue . . .

The Landlord: Ah, yes, two stalwart officers of the law sworn to protect their fellow man. But who are those crowding around them?

Gabriel: Young idealists, sir, dedicated to social justice. Now, listen. Hear what they're shouting? "Pigs! Pigs! Pigs!"

The Landlord (aghast): And they're throwing bricks at those two policemen—trying to maim those two children of God!

Gabriel: Oh, no, sir. Not children of God. Pigs. The demonstrators have transformed them into pigs and can now maim them in good conscience.

The Landlord: I see. And that big soldier over there in Vietnam shooting at a fleeing old woman? Has he changed her into a pig, too?

Gabriel: No, sir. He changed her into a gook, a dink or a slope. It was easy. She didn't speak his language. Nor was she familiar with his customs. That always makes the magic easier.

The Landlord (Sadly): Transforming the children of God into pigs and gooks. How tragic!

Gabriel: Oh, not only pigs and gooks, sir, but nips and wops and krauts and chinks. For example, they never lynch a fellow man until they have turned him into a nigger or a coon.

The Landlord (shaking his head): It's blasphemous.

Gabriel (gleefully raising his trumpet): Shall I blow, sir, and wipe these scum from the face of your Earth?

The Landlord (his brow darkening): These what, Gabriel?

Gabriel (ranting): Those rats! That trash! These sc. . . . (suddenly lowering his trumpet, crestfallen) Oh, forgive me, sir. I'm no better than they.

The Landlord (in a voice of thunder): Never forget, Gabriel, that he who would transform a child of God into something less than human is an accessory to murder!

6

EUROPEAN MAGAZINES
PEEKARAMA
EXOTIC ART MOVIES
53
ADULT STAG SHO
SEXUAL FANTASI
DEMONSTRATED
MEN AND WOM
UTHENTIC
SHOW YOUR
Y BACK IF YOU
SEE ACTION
THE STAG MASTER
GET A FREE PEEK
OF SHOW IN LOBBY
NEW SHOW TUES
nimal Lover
COMING SOON!

Sex

Long May It Rave

Is Sex Old-Fashioned?

Once upon a time there was a young lad named Horatio Alger, who was determined to struggle and persevere and somehow get himself a good education. A good sex education.

But the little lad faced many hurdles. The first was the local school board, which voted 5-4 against showing Horatio any sex education films. The second was Horatio's parents, who voted 2-0 against allowing Horatio to attend any Adult Movies.

"Adult movies," thundered Horatio's father, "are corrupting the morals of our youth and destroying our American way of life."

So Horatio was 18 and on his own before he saw his first Adult Movie. He didn't, of course, understand it. But he thrust forth his chin and vowed to persevere.

For two years, Horatio persevered. He saw Adult Movies thrice weekly and twice on Saturdays. "It was a hard struggle," he said proudly on reaching 20, "but at last I have won myself a good sex education."

It was then he met Miss Penelope Trueheart and fell in love.

"All I desire on this earth," he said, falling to his knees one night in her apartment, "is to be the father of your child and spend the rest of my life as your husband."

"Oh, dearest," said Miss Trueheart ecstatically, "when will we be married?"

"As soon as we have a child," said Horatio, drawing on his good sex education. "For we can't have one afterward, you know. People never do."

"And how do we have a child?" she asked, blushing modestly.

"There are several ways," said Horatio. "The easiest, I believe, is for you to smoke a cigarette on the couch. I will pounce on you. Your hand will go limp and the cigarette will fall on the carpet. (We can use an ashtray, I suppose, if you worry about fire.) And then you will cry."

"I don't smoke," said Miss Trueheart.

"Then we'll have to throw our clothes on the floor," said Horatio, "though it isn't very tidy. But please turn up the heat first as we have to lie under just a sheet and talk. Then I will go for a drive and you will cry."

"Will you take me in your arms, dearest?" she asked hesitantly.

"Yes," said Horatio. "In the shower."

"I don't have a shower," said Miss Trueheart, close to tears.

"Well, I guess we can skip that," said Horatio dubiously, as he threw his tie on the floor. "Come, my love, I can hardly wait."

So they threw their clothes on the floor, got under the sheet, talked and then Horatio dressed and went for a drive while Miss Trueheart cried.

But, oddly enough, though they faithfully repeated this routine every night for seven years, they never did have a child.

With his good sex education, Horatio privately blamed

Miss Trueheart for neither smoking nor having a shower. But he was too gallant to say so.

Moral: Adult Movies may, indeed, destroy our way of life. And the human race along with it.

Keep Sex Dirty

Herewith is another unwritten chapter from that unpublished text, A History of the World, 1950 to 1999. Its title: "The Dirty Sex Drive."

By the late 1960s the public was well on the way to being emancipated from what was usually referred to as its "Victorian hang-ups" on sex.

Ladies of fashion were using four-letter words in mixed company. Movies were franker than ever. And to liberalize public attitudes even further, crusades were being launched under such slogans as, "Support Necrophilia between Consenting Adults."

A breakthrough came in the mid-seventies with the historic Dread Sot Decision. This involved a foreign film which depicted a 143-minute drunken carnal orgy with a 30-second shot of a leaf fluttering to the ground.

The courts held the film did not appeal "solely to prurient interests" as there was obviously something in it for botanists and other leaf lovers. And so the last taboos were shattered.

Psychologists, sociologists and philosophers were ecstatic.

"At last," they said, "mankind has rid himself of his age-old fears and complexes about sex. At last, he will have the same healthy attitudes toward sex as he has toward, say, jogging."

And they proved absolutely right. The public came to look on sex precisely as it had looked upon jogging. The effects were disastrous.

First hit were the foreign art films. Who wanted to watch 143 minutes of uninterrupted jogging? And they were attended only by dedicated botanists hopeful of catching a glimpse of a falling leaf.

Topless reviews went bust. Bottomless reviews hit bottom. Playboy merged with the Evergreen Review. And the unemployment rate on Madison avenue, where voyeurism had been the prime stock in trade, reached 67.3 per cent. The economy tottered.

Worst of all, precisely the same proportion of the public now practiced sex as had practiced jogging—.08 per cent.

Ladies conceded it was obviously a healthy, stimulating activity—but it absolutely ruined their hair-dos.

Gentlemen admitted that it was sure good for the old waistline and had its pleasurable effects—but it was sweaty, untidy and definitely undignified.

And thus the future of the human race hung in the balance.

It was saved by the DAR, which had never given up. Secretly financed by the movie houses, the magazine magnates and Madison avenue tycoons, the DAR launched a massive Dirty Sex Drive under the slogan: "Cherish the Heritage of Our Forefathers—Make Sex Dirty Again."

"Sex is illicit?" cried the ladies, a blush on their cheeks.

"Sex is dirty?" cried the gentlemen, a gleam in their eye.

Once again adultery flourished, love nests were bared, voyeurism thrived, the economy prospered and humanity survived.

A similar attempt by The President's Physical Fitness Committee to create a salacious and licentious image of jogging in the public mind—for reasons not yet determined by sociologists—failed dismally.

A Bold Advance In Television

The founding of a new television network "to meet the unmet needs of the viewing public" was announced yesterday. It will be known as the Fun Broadcasting System.

FBS President Greeley Grommet said that present network programming was "gravely out of balance" and that it was the duty of public broadcasters to "satisfy the tastes of all television viewers.

"Today we have violent shows for those who like violence," he said. "We have comedy shows for those who like comedy. We have dramatic shows for those who like drama. And we have educational television for those who like to watch two Jewish doctors arguing with each other.

"But what does television offer today," he said, "to those who like sex?"

Grommet conceded that the networks had taken some strides forward in recent years toward meeting the need. He cited the jokes on Laugh-In and a shaving commercial as examples.

But, he said, there could be no question that television lagged far behind all other media in fulfilling its obligations in this field.

"We have dirty books, dirty movies, dirty magazines and dirty plays," he said. "But nowhere can one watch dirty television."

Grommet said that FBS initially would confine its programming to old dirty movies.

"We feel that we will be providing a valuable service to the deprived shut-in who can't get down to his neighborhood dirty movie house," he said.

"But within a year," he said, "we hope to provide a wide range of dirty programs that will appeal to all dirty tastes."

Programs now under consideration by FBS, he said, include a quiz show ("I've Got a Dirty Secret"), a literary program ("Dirty Books and Dirty Authors"), and an Ed Sullivan-type talent extravaganza ("Saturday Night Orgy").

As for a dramatic series, Grommet said FBS was attempting to acquire the rights to Peyton Place. "We'll simply refilm it to show what happened off camera," he explained.

The 6 o'clock news, he said, would include the day's major sex crimes, tastefully photographed, and the usual feature stories, such as "Strange Sex Habits around the World."

"We will also, of course, devote the required number of hours to public service programs as specified by FCC regulations," he said. "One such will be 'Learn through Play and Lose Weight.' This will combine audio-visual sex education aids for the kiddies with interesting exercises for the flabby."

Grommet conceded that FBS was expecting "a few complaints" from viewers.

"Our market studies show that approximately the same number of people dislike sex as dislike violence," he said. "Of course, they can simply switch to another channel that caters to their hang-up."

Grommet was asked if FBS wouldn't be pandering to the very lowest common denominator of the American public taste.

"Exactly," he said happily. "And that's why we confidently predict the highest ratings in television history."

Sexual Equality Now!

Growing discontent among the Nation's largest oppressed minority group was long evident to skilled observers. But few were prepared for the full-scale riots that broke out in the spring of 1970.

Chief fomenter of the revolt was Benny Freedman, author of "The Male Mystique" and founder of the militant Men's Liberation Front. Its battle cry: "Sexual Equality for All—Freedom Now!"

Progress toward sexual equality in this country had been agonizingly slow. For example, it wasn't until 1968 that Vassar, that bastion of femininity, was at last integrated—and then with only a few "token males."

By the mid-sixties some male militants were wearing their hair in shoulder-length "naturals" and adopting the gay colors in dress hitherto reserved for women. In their battle for equality, a few went so far as to take on "the unisex look"—despite snickers and snide looks from women everywhere.

But it was Freedman who lit the fuse. In an article in Look magazine entitled, "The Rage of Men," he cited an incendiary statistic: Although men comprise two-thirds of the Nation's labor force, women spend and control 70 per cent of the country's private wealth.

"Moreover," wrote an angry Freedman, "women not only take the cushier jobs, such as teaching, library management and stenography, but they have forced through discriminatory legislation providing themselves with shorter working hours, special lounges and extra coffee breaks.

"Who digs the ditches, mines the coal and hauls the garbage? Who lifts that load and totes that bale? Who gets all the menial, backbreaking, degrading jobs in our society? The oppressed minority of men, that's who."

But Freedman reserved most of his wrath for "the insidious double standard in sexual relationships."

"From the age of 13 or 14 when the male first deals with the opposite sex, he is inculcated in this double standard. If he goes to the movies with a female, he must not only buy his own ticket, but hers, too.

"As he grows older, he must light her cigarettes, open the door for her, hold her coat and leap respectfully to his feet when she enters the room. Should she strike him, he may not even strike back. Surely, no slave on an ante-bellum plantation was ever more humiliated daily.

"Thus we see that persecuted and overworked men can look forward to only a shorter life expectancy, while coddled women look forward to a world cruise on the insurance policies they have forced their poor husbands to buy.

"Even in death," concluded Freedman, "there is no escape from sexual injustice!"

The inflammatory article was passed around in such male ghettoes as the Elks Club and the YMCA.

Arrests mounted as angry men stormed boutiques, salons and debutante teas. Freedom Riders caused riots in their attempts to integrate the separate-but-equal facilities in bus depots across the land. There were parades and sit-ins and a March on Washington.

At last, the First Lady herself, who had quietly run the country from behind the scenes, appeared on nationwide television to point out that women comprised 51 per cent of the population and to appeal for "faith in the democratic process."

"Sexual equality is certainly a goal to strive for," she said, expressing what was in the hearts of so many. "But men just aren't ready for it."

The Hottest Book In Sex Education

Good news! The forward-looking Southern Baptists, meeting in Nashville, have voted to give sex education courses in their churches based on "a sound Biblical approach."

This is a wise step. There is certainly no better textbook for a sex education course than the Bible.

We'll pass over the Song of Solomon here, mainly because we can't reprint the text in a family newspaper. But let us envision a typical happy, eager Sunday School Sex Education Class.

Miss Primm: Now that we all understand begatting, are there any questions, children?

Johnny: How old was Methuselah when he begat Lamech?

Miss Primm: He was 187, Johnny.

Johnny: Wow! What's next, Miss Primm?

Miss Primm: Wife swapping, Johnny. Let us turn to Genesis 12:15 and read how Abraham swapped his wife, Sarai, who "was very fair," to the Pharaoh of Egypt.

Billie: Did the Pharaoh give him his wife in return?

Miss Primm: No, Billie, he gave Abram "sheep, and oxen, and he asses, and menservants, and maidservants, and she asses, and camels."

Billie: Man, what a groovy deal! I'm going to get married when I grow up.

Miss Primm (pleased): I'm so glad, Billie. One thing we want to learn in Sunday school is the values of matrimony.

Billie (nodding enthusiastically): It sure beats swapping bubble-gum cards.

Miss Primm: And the other is the values of having a family. Now if you'll all turn to Genesis 19:8 we'll read about how Lot and his two beautiful daughters were surrounded in their house in Sodom by a mob of angry sex fiends.

Millicent: Oooo, Miss Primm, what did poor Lot do?

Miss Primm: Why, he bravely stepped out the door and addressed them, saying—let's see here—"Behold now, I have two daughters which have not known man; let me, I pray you, bring them out unto you, and do ye to them as is good in your eyes."

Johnny: You mean what's good in a sex fiend's eyes? Boy, that's socko, Miss Primm. What's next?

Miss Primm: Incest, Johnny. You see, Lot and his daughters escape to a cave and the older daughter says to the younger (Genesis 19:32): "Come, let us make our father drink wine, and we will lie with him, that we may preserve the seed of our father." Now you can read the lurid details yourselves. The story ends: "Thus were both the daughters of Lot with child by their father." That's all for today, class.

Billie: Gosh, Miss Primm, what will we study next week?

Miss Primm: Mass orgies. We'll begin with Numbers 31:8–42 which describes how Moses and the Israelites defeated the Midianites, slew all the men, gave the women gynecological examinations and kept 32,000 virgins for their sport.

Johnnie: Man o' man, Miss Primm, Sunday school sure is fun!

So, hats off, I say, to the Southern Baptists for coming up with a brand new textbook on sex education only several thousand years old.

Of course, there will be some prudes who'll contend that such material has no place in our Nation's churches. Let's pray the Baptists don't get themselves arrested.

A Successful Course

The publication of "Human Sexual Inadequacy" by Masters and Johnson in April of 1970 created a nationwide stir.

The work was the result of 20 years of research by the two respected scientists at their Reproductive Biology Clinic in St. Louis. There they had been giving couples courses in sexual attitudes and techniques with classroom seminars and plenty of homework.

Newspaper accounts of the clinic had their most immediate impact on the campus of Skarewe University. The students, having created a Black Studies Program, kicked out all corporate recruiters, abolished ROTC and blown up the statue of General Skidmore Skarewe as an example of male chauvinism, had just tied up Dean Grommet again and were wondering what to demand next.

"Hey, listen to this!" cried SDS President Jack Armstrong, waving a paper. "In St. Louis they've got a kind of College of Sexual Knowledge. Man, does that ever sound relevant!"

Dean Grommet said, on his gag being removed, what wise deans say these days. He said he thought it was a fine idea. The following week the Sex Studies Program was launched at Skarewe University.

It was a smashing success. No less than 92.4 per cent of the student body promptly enrolled in the four-year program leading to a B.S. or Bachelor of Sex degree. Classes were appallingly overcrowded but no one complained.

The faculty was enthusiastic. "Never in 30 years teaching," said a newly appointed professor of erogenous zones, "have I seen students so attentive in class nor so diligent in their homework."

There were naturally some protests from stuffy parents. Imagine the shock of Hiram Dootey, on paying a surprise visit to his daughter's dorm, to find her preparing a position paper on Interesting Far East Positions with the help of a young male classmate.

"But golly, Daddy," said young Daphne Dootey indignantly, "when it comes to preparing myself for life this makes more sense than Etruscan funeral orations. I just want to make some man the best wife in the world."

"Couldn't you take cooking and sewing instead?" suggested Mr. Dootey weakly.

"Who wants the best sewing wife in the world?" replied Daphne. "I want to be the best . . ."

"Daphne!" cried her father, retiring in defeat.

The change in campus attitudes was dramatic. Grinds, hitherto sneered at, were now the most popular. While a higher percentage of students broke down from overwork, the rewards of good study habits were gratifying. Daphne, on graduating magna cum laude, received 373 proposals from all over the world—two of them for marriage.

No one was happier than Dean Grommet. There hadn't been a riot since the program began. Some ascribed this to the student body's daily listlessness. But the Dean saw higher meaning.

"For years we tried to interest the students in the subjects we offered," he said, "instead of offering the one subject that interested them. No wonder we failed."

"But teaching them only sex . . ." said a trustee, frowning.

"Good heavens," said the Dean, surprised. "What else did they ever learn in college, anyway?"

Let Us Build A Gay New World

"I think it can be proven that there has never been a single birth from a homosexual union"—Professor George Argyres, the noted population expert.

"Look Doctor, I might as well say it right out. I think I'm . . . I think I'm a queer."

"Just make yourself comfortable on the couch, Mr. Portnoy. But please don't use that word. In psychiatry, we prefer the term, 'heterosexual inclinations.' "

"Yeah, okay, Doc, whatever. But I've got this thing about girls. I mean I like girls."

"Well, now, Mr. Portnoy, it's not the end of the world. Thirty years ago, before the discovery of The Argyres Effect, most adult males were practicing heterosexuals."

"The Argyres Effect?"

"That's right. He discovered that only heterosexuals reproduce. At the time, mankind was on the brink of being snuffed out at any minute by a population explosion. His discovery was electrifying. Almost overnight, heterosexuality became the worst sort of anti-social behavior."

"That's amazing, Doc."

"Not really. Cultural mores reflect social needs. When the world was underpopulated and societies wanted more births, homosexuality was abhorred. It was logical that the moral standards became reversed when the needs of society were reversed."

"Thanks for the history lesson, Doc. But what about me? I mean I've met this girl who's . . . Well, Jane's a heterosexual, too. And we've—well, we're secretly living together. You won't tell, will you?"

"Professional ethics aside, I wouldn't anyway, Mr. Portnoy. As a tolerant man, I firmly support proposed legislation that would allow heterosexual acts in private between consenting adults."

"Oh, Jane and I never hold hands in public or make a spectacle of ourselves. Occasionally, we'll go to this little straight bar we know about where heteros dance together. And sometimes we'll sneak into this dirty movie theater, which shows boys and girls kissing and hug . . ."

"There's no need to go into sordid details, Mr. Portnoy."

"But if it ever gets out, Doc, I'd lose my job. My folks'd die of shame. It would be the end of everything."

"Now, now, Mr. Portnoy. I know of several cases where heterosexuals have been rehabilitated to lead productive lives. You must think of your aberration, not as a failing, but as a sickness."

"But the thing is, Doc. I like liking girls. And I . . . You might as well know it, I love Jane."

"Look here, Portnoy. Pull yourself together. What kind of a world would this be if everyone were heterosexual? Men would be clubbing each other and marching off to wars again to prove their masculinity to the opposite sex. Once again, we'd have a population explosion. Wars, violence, famine, pestilence—those are the fruits of heterosexuality."

"I know, Doctor, I'm sorry. But the thing is . . . My real problem is that Jane and I . . . I mean . . . Look, I've got to tell somebody. Janeisgoingtohaveababy!"

"A what! Good Lord, Portnoy, you don't need a psychiatrist. You need a lawyer. Oh, you'll be lucky to get off with 20 years. You know how society feels about couples who perform unnatural sex acts."

The End of Free Love

Nothing angers decent Americans more than the thought of welfare mothers spawning welfare children. They are blamed for soaring welfare costs, the unbalanced budget, overpopulation and the rise in purse snatchings.

This is surprising. The solution to the problem was invented a full decade ago by the noted mechanical engineer, Lou W. Free:

A fool-proof, fully-automatic, coin-operated chastity belt.

The belt operates on the same simple principle as the parking meter: It is activated by a coin and when the time is up, a violation is signaled. (With the belt, however, violations are expected to be rare.) And, as with the parking meter, all revenue will be collected by the government.

The initial purpose of the device, like the parking meter, was to increase the government income. It has been calculated that once every woman is equipped with one, the federal budget will show a $6.3 billion surplus in the first year—even at rates as low as ten cents a half hour.

As of now, the government taxes eating, drinking, gambling, traveling, telephoning, marrying, fishing, dying and being amused. The coin-operated chastity belt would simply allow the government to tax the last remaining untaxed activity.

Surely no decent American, with the budget hanging in the balance, could object to that.

But in addition to creating the first budget surplus in years, the belt will deal firmly with the basic problem of welfare—the poor mothers who go right on having poor children just as though they could afford them.

It is not, of course, the actual having of the child that angers all decent Americans. A child is a blessed event.

What angers all decent Americans is the poor heedlessly indulging in the activity that leads to motherhood. Why should decent American taxpayers support such licentious pleasures?

Up to now, however, they have found no legal way to curtail the blind selfishness of the poor. The coin-operated chastity belt is the obvious answer. Henceforth, the luxuriant joy of physical love will be restricted to those who can afford to pay for it.

We don't indulge the poor in yachting, polo or rare book collecting. These are pleasures every decent American earns by hard work, grit or inheritence. Why should we indulge the poor in this?

When it comes to the poor—and I'm sure every decent American deep in his heart agrees—it's much too good for them.

Time forbids enumerating all the fringe benefits that will accrue once all women are equiped with coin-operated chastity belts.

Suffice it to say that free love, which outrages all decent Americans, will become a thing of the past. And in turn, overpopulation will be curbed—it being surprising what people will do solely because it's free.

There will be frustrations, of course, as any man who has ever approached a parking meter with nothing smaller than a $10 bill can testify.

But these are the frustrations of modern life. Surely every decent American will find these a small price to pay for balancing the budget, ending free love, curbing overpopulation and, above all, denying poor people unearned pleasures.

Indeed, it is difficult to conceive of a device more symbolic of every decent American's deepest aspirations.

All Us Pigs Are Equal

Once upon a time there was a Typical American Housewife named Gwendolyn Gwen, who worried.

Like most women for a million years or so, she worried about raising her children and feeding her husband and fixing up her home and things like that.

Like most women for a million years or so, she believed in peace and sobriety and constancy and gentleness and things like that.

Her husband, George, was a Typical American Male. He worked too hard and drank too much and didn't spend enough time with the kids and often chased the ladies and sometimes pushed people around and things like that.

But they thought they were happy with their lot.

Then, one day, Gwendolyn ran into an old high school chum named Lavona Laganape. Lavona was Sergeant at Arms of the Women Against Male Mastery, better known as WAMM!

Lavona took one look at Gwendolyn, sniffed and said loudly, "Gwendolyn, you are a slave! Follow me and get yourself liberated."

So Gwendolyn went to a WAMM! meeting. She learned that she was no more than an unpaid charwoman, cook and baby-sitter. Which didn't sound fair.

She learned she didn't have equal rights under the law. Which didn't sound fair. Wouldn't have an equal shot at the top jobs in any profession. Which didn't sound fair. And couldn't get equal pay for equal work. Which sounded outrageous.

So Gwendolyn joined WAMM!, read every word Betty

Friedan ever wrote, took an eight-week course in karate, went home and told George to make his own breakfast because she was now liberated.

When George, in typical male fashion, sneered, Gwendolyn called him a "male chauvinist pig!" and gave him a karate chop to the brisket. George, who didn't even know judo, decided to take this lying down.

Gwendolyn put the kids in a day care center, got a job that paid as much as George's and spent her free hours marching militantly around shouting, "Male chauvinist pigs!"

Of course, society changes slowly. It took years before men grudgingly gave women equal rights.

And during those years Gwendolyn, to show she was the equal of any man, took up smoking cigars and drinking her whiskey neat and cussing and having an affair with her male secretary and things like that.

Naturally, she didn't have much time for the kids any more. And, naturally, she didn't talk much about peace or gentleness. But sacrifices have to be made for a worthy cause. And at last victory was theirs.

At last, women had equal rights, equal pay and equal opportunities. Lavona gave a party to celebrate.

Unfortunately, George caught Gwendolyn, who'd had a few too many, pinching the bartender. They had an awful fight—ten rounds, no holds barred. It ended in a draw.

"At last I can say truthfully," cried Gwendolyn triumphantly, scattering cigar ashes on the rug as she woozily poured herself another belt, "that I'm the bleeping equal of any bleeping male chauvinist pig in the room!"

Moral: The trouble with women becoming our equals, gentlemen, is that then they'll be no better than we are.

7

Government

My Country, Sane or Otherwise

Who'll Die for Gluch?

Once upon a time there was a country called Gluch. It was unique among all the countries of the world. It was unique because not a single solitary Gluchian was patriotic.

No one owned a Gluchian flag. No one knew the words to the Gluchian national anthem. And no one had ever died for Gluch. In fact, the whole idea was ridiculous.

On the rare occasions when some screwball would cry out: "Forward men, to do or die for Gluch!" people would start snickering. "Die for Gluch?" they'd say. And they'd slap their thighs. And pretty soon they'd be rolling on the ground, holding their sides.

Conversely, no imperialistic neighbor ever even tried to conquer Gluch. "Who," as Charlemagne the Great put it in 803 A.D., "wants to be known as the Conqueror of Gluch?"

So Gluch dwelt in peace. Every four years a lottery was held to select a new Glumph (or King) of Gluch. Naturally, no one wanted to be known by such a dumb title. So the loser of the lottery, moaning piteously, got the job.

The duties of the Glumph of Gluch were to enforce the law and collect taxes. There being no legislature to pass laws, there weren't any laws. And there being no Army, Navy, Department of Highways, or Gluchian National Band, there weren't any taxes to collect, either.

So you can see why Gluch had no patriots. It had nothing to be patriotic about. It was neither rich nor powerful nor feared nor envied. In fact, patriots from rich and powerful countries thought of Gluch as kind of a joke.

Well, this couldn't last. One day a spellbinder named Spencer Spellbinder rose up. "Let us change the name of our country from Gluch," he said with fiendish cleverness, "to the United Republic of Goldenland!"

"Why?" asked a little boy.

"Because young men will march off to do or die for Goldenland!" explained Spellbinder. "Then we can seize Spitzbergen, Siam and Schenectady."

"Who needs them?" asked an old man.

"We will become rich and powerful and feared and envied!" cried Spellbinder. "We will have the biggest Army and the strongest Navy and the most freeways, telephones, airports, television antennae and topless dancers of any country in the whole world!"

"Whatever for?" asked a sweet young thing.

"Why," said Spellbinder, somewhat surprised, "so that we can all take pride in our country as true patriots, of course."

For the first and only time in the history of Gluch the citizens were roused to action. Their first action was to ride Spellbinder out of the country on a rail.

Their second was to change the nation's name from Gluch to Gludge—on the grounds that it should prove even more difficult to die for Gludge than Gluch.

The Gludgians then lived happily ever after.

Moral: It's fun to be a patriot, but it's better to love your country.

The President Who Went Crackers

It was on March 4, 1973—just two months into his first term of office—that the President of the United States went crackers.

The loyalty of his staff, like all White House staffs, was first of all to the President. Naturally, they agreed immediately that the fact he was nuttier than a fruitcake must be kept from the public at all costs.

For several months all went well. The President occupied himself cutting out and trying on paper crowns and miters. The staff issued the requisite number of innocuous statements on current affairs. And it was six months before people began saying, "Funny, don't think I've seen the President lately."

Something had to be done. The staff waited for a day the President believed himself to be Marie Antoinette. They then had him confront a staff member on nationwide television.

"Mr. President," said the staff member carefully, "poor families on the surplus food program are currently receiving only chick peas and lard."

"Let them," said the President grandly, "eat cake."

The reaction to including a Sara Lee Fudge Cake in every food package was predictable.

Those who had voted for the President because of his broad smile or his political party, called it "a humanitarian gesture that spells the end of hunger in America."

Those who had voted against him because of his close-set eyes or his political party, called it "an act of welfare coddling that will further sap this nation's moral fiber."

A Gallup Poll showed 53.2 per cent approved of the way the President was handling his job.

Six months later, the staff was forced to act again. They picked a day when the President thought he was Mahatma Gandhi and asked him on nationwide television his views on war and peace.

Unfortunately, ten seconds before air time, the President had transmogrified into Napoleon Bonaparte. He thus twirled the globe by his desk, stuck a pin in it and cried, "Allons, mes enfants!" (Meaning, "Let's go, kids!")

As luck would have it, the pin hit Ugulap Islands, an atoll in the Southwest Mbongan Sea inhabited by 27 aborigines and a duck-billed platypus.

Again, public reaction split over the subsequent American invasion. The New Left sewed up Ugulap flags, decried "Wall Street oil barons" and smashed 32 drug store windows to halt "Capitalist exploitation of indigenous social struggles."

Pro-Administration columnists and congressmen defended the move on the grounds that "as Ugulap goes, so goes the Mbongan Sea." Most intellectuals also approved the President's statement because he said it in French.

In Peoria, Ohio, however, a small boy watched the President on television and innocently asked, "How come the President's a cuckoo-eyed loony?"

But no one listens to small boys, except their mothers. This one's mother washed his mouth out with soap. And 54.6 per cent of the public said they approved of the way the President was handling his job.

Fortunately, at the end of four years he regained his sanity and was easily re-elected. Public approval of the way he was handling his job remained about the same during his second term as it had during his first.

The Conglomerated States of America

It was on June 30, 1984—New Fiscal Year's Eve—that General Everything, Inc., announced its merger with the United States Government.

There was, of course, some opposition to this last of the giant mergers. Old-fashioned patriots accused the Government of "getting panicky and selling out." And some General Everything stockholders protested that taking over a mismanaged concern with $1.2 trillion in liabilities was far too risky a venture.

But in his historic Declaration of Interdependence, General Everything's President, Grocker Grommet, pointed out that the Government also had numerous assets, both liquid and frozen.

"Let us not forget that it was courage and vision that made General Everything what it is today," said the man who was to become known as The Father of His Conglomerate. "By installing a dynamic new management and instituting sound business principles, we foresee a high growth potential for this newest of our subsidiaries."

For the average citizen, life in the Conglomerated States of America was a change for the better.

Like all modern businesses, the Conglomerate's health and welfare plans were far superior to the old Medicare and O.E.O programs. And the retirement benefits were double those of Social Security.

School children quickly learned the new Pledge of Allegiance to "one Conglomerate, under sound business management, indivisible, with high corporate profits for all."

Unemployment and poverty soon became a thing of the past. For, as President Grommet said, "Idle workers are a deplorable waste of manpower and represent an increased cost factor of 3.7 percent per shift. Such inefficiency will no longer be tolerated."

The Conglomerate built modern company housing, modern company recreation facilities and modern company towns for its employees. And as every citizen was an employee of the Conglomerate, all enjoyed modern company living.

The war in Vietnam was liquidated 13 days after the merger. Market Research reported that Vietnam was, at best, "a marginal sales territory." And Cost Accounting calculated that, at best, it would take 207 years to recoup the Conglomerate's annual $30 billion investment in the war.

So the employees of The Conglomerated States of America dwelt in peace and plenty. And while some missed poets, Fourth of July parades, hippies and the Democratic national convention, most agreed that the new-found security and material well-being were worth these losses.

Unfortunately, in May of 1996, the Conglomerate became overextended in a Bolivian saltpeter mine. The resultant shock waves rippled through its holdings.

The Conglomerate's stock plummeted 93 points on the Conglomerate's stock exchange. President Grommet leapt from a window of the Washington Monument. And the Conglomerate States of America went bankrupt.

It was purchased for three cents on the dollar by The League for Creeping Socialism.

The League immediately nationalized all private holdings, built modern Government housing, recreation facilities and towns, and re-instituted Government-run health, welfare and retirement programs.

Oddly enough, citizens of the new Socialized States of America couldn't tell the difference.

Mr. Nixon Finds a Southern Justice

Washington, D.C., February 7, 1972—The White House today announced the nomination of Justice of the Peace Appleton Shote of Soowee county, Georgia, to the long-vacant seat on the U.S. Supreme Court.

Administration sources described Shote as "a moderate Southerner and a genuine constructionist."

Attorney General John Mitchell, who personally conducted the six-month investigation of Shote's background, said he was confident of "speedy Senate approval" of the nomination.

"My exhaustive inquiries have not disclosed one shred of evidence that Mr. Shote has ever accepted a consultant's fee, owned stock, suffered a conflict of interest, made a racist speech, or owned a segregated golf course," Mitchell said. "I'm glad the three-year search is over."

The nomination was hailed by Shote's friends and neighbors in Soowee county. "It's the best thing that ever happened to Sowee county," said one, "if'n it means that shiftless skunk'll be moving to Washington."

News of the nomination was broken to Shote by reporters, who found him on the banks of the Sowbelly river, sipping White Lightning from a Mason jar.

At first, Shote expressed some hesitation on accepting the nomination to the Nation's highest court. "What's this here job pay," he inquired, "and what are the hours?"

On being told, Shote said he reckoned he'd take it—"leastwise till I start drawing my Social Security come next January."

A reporter asked Shote if he considered himself "a genuine constructionist."

"Well, now," he replied, "I did help Mrs. Purdy up Twin Forks way shore up her privy after the big storm in '32, but I ain't done much in that line since."

Another inquired about Shote's views on the Constitution. "My liver's right fine and the ticker's beating like a $50 watch," said Shote, "and though I've been a mite gassy in the belly lately 'taint worth paying no never mind."

The reporters then began digging in Shote's past. But after two hours of probing, they had to admit the White House had at last come up with a Southern candidate without a blemish on his record.

Or, as Shote truthfully put it, lifting himself up on one elbow, "Hell, boys, I ain't never done nothing at all."

An enterprising Life magazine reporter at this point whipped out a contract. "Read this, sir," he said eagerly. "Life will pay you $50,000, if you'll write your first-person account of how you became the perfect Southern nominee to the Supreme Court."

"Read?" said Shote, blinking slowly. "Write?"

The White House late today withdrew Shote's nomination and said the search for a qualified Southerner would continue.

A delegation of Southern leaders, headed by Senator Strom Thurmond, called on the President this evening and asked him to nominate a Northerner instead.

"Mr. Nixon's pig-headed determination to nominate a Southerner," angrily explained Senator Thurmond later, "is giving the South a bad name."

Jed Garoover, Crime Fighter!

Hi, there, tee-vee fans. Hold on to your hats 'cause off we go on a brand new adventure serial—Jed Garoover, Crime Fighter!

It's the exciting, thrilling story of how Jed Garoover carries on his one-man crusade against America's enemies with unrelenting vigor—even though he's 104 years old.

As we join Jed today he's in his humble 20-room suite of offices atop the Washington Monument conferring with his young secretary, Lotus Lane. She's only 96.

Jed: All right, Miss Lane, let me have your daily report on the evil doings of America's greatest enemies.

Miss Lane (reading from a list): Well, Chief, first of all, one of your agents stubbed his toe while pursuing a bank robber and in his pain exclaimed, according to sworn affadavits by three fellow agents, "Good Garoover!"

Jed (shocked): That's a clear case of taking my name in vain. To Boise with him! Will these young whippersnappers in my Bureau never learn the discipline required to preserve our cherished American freedoms? What else, Miss Lane?

Miss Lane: There's Congress, Chief. It seems . . .

Jed (thoughtfully): Ah, yes, it's budget time again. Issue routine orders to all agents to discover a conspiracy so that our friends in Congress will unanimously increase our appropriations as usual. Let's see in recent years we've discovered the Old Red Conspiracy, the New Black Conspiracy and the Young White Conspiracy. Hmmm. What about a Yellow Conspiracy this year to brighten things up? Check our files on Oriental-Americans, Miss Lane.

Miss Lane: Yes, Chief. But there's something else a few Congressmen want from you.

Jed (complacently): Anything for my dear friends in Congress. What is it?

Miss Lane (hesitantly): Your resignation. Chief.

Jed (stunned): You mean there are actually enemies of America in Congress? This is the worst conspiracy I ever heard of!

Miss Lane: They say, Chief—forgive them, they know not what they do—that you're too old.

Jed: Too old? Why, I don't feel a day over a hundred. I can still better down a door with my shoulder, just as always. Watch! (He totters across the room, misses the door and hits the window which, fortunately doesn't break.) Don't stand there, Miss Lane, pick me up!

Miss Lane (picking him up): Oh, Chief, I'm worried!

Jed (grimly): Don't worry, Miss Lane. I can still shoot as straight as ever. I'll gun down these dirty rats who would destroy America by getting me to retire. Toss me my trusty pistol, Miss Lane. I'll show them I'm as young as ever.

Miss Lane (happily): Oh, Chief, I just know you will. (She tosses him his pistol which catches him in the breadbasket).

Jed (testily): Well, don't just stand there, Miss Lane, pick me up again!

Will Jed Garoover retire while still in the prime of his second century? Will the Good Lord quit making green apples? Be sure to tune in again next time, folks, for the further thrilling adventures of our popular 104-year-old Crime Fighter.

And, now, a word from Geritol . . .

The Admirer of Law and Order

Once upon a time there was a little boy whose friends called him "Dolf." Dolf was a very good little boy, who did everything his mother and his father and his teachers told him to do. He even kept his room straight.

"I want to do what I'm told," said little Dolf, "because, above all else, I want to be good." And his mother and his father and his teachers all agreed he was very, very good.

Of course, occasionally he fell into bad company. Once, in his student days he met an Anarchist who told him the Anarchist creed:

"Always do what's right, even though the authorities forbid it; never do what's wrong, even though the authorities require it."

Young Dolf was shocked. "But society depends on obedience to its laws and respect for order," he protested. "You can't have people deciding for themselves which laws they'll obey and which orders they won't. Why, that way lies anarchy!"

So Dolf grew up to be a very, very good citizen who believed, above all else, in law and order.

Unfortunately, the Nation was suffering from a terrible malaise. There were riots and arson and all kinds of agitators went around disobeying laws and creating disorder.

The people grew pretty sick and tired of this and demanded a return to law and order. And a man came along who promised them just that. So they elected him their leader.

Dolf was very happy. "Now we can all be good citizens and respect the laws and obey the orders of the authorities," he said. And everybody did. Because everybody who didn't was shot.

Privately, Dolf wasn't too happy about that. But because he believed so deeply in law and order, he had risen to a trusted post in the government. And it was his job to help carry out the Leader's laws and orders.

"But after all," he said, "you can't have people deciding for themselves which laws they'll obey. That way lies anarchy!" So he carried out the laws.

Then the Leader blamed all the Nation's troubles on scheming malcontents in the ghettoes. And he issued orders to wipe these troublemakers out.

Privately, Dolf wasn't too happy about that, either. "But after all," he said, "you can't have people deciding for themselves which orders they won't obey. That way lies anarchy!"

And sure enough, thanks to the Leader's stern measures, the Nation became the most lawful and orderly country in the whole, wide world.

Unfortunately, it got in a war, lost and Dolf was captured. He was even put on trial. Naturally, he was flabbergasted.

"But I'm the last person to be accused of any crime," he said. "I was the most dutiful of citizens, who obeyed every law and followed every order. I am therefore good."

But the world disagreed. And because he had obeyed every law and followed every order, Adolf Eichmann was hanged by the neck until he was dead.

Moral: the Anarchists are right.

The Humiliation of Victor J. Very

Victor J. Very awakened early in his modest three-bedroom tax shelter. As was his custom, he yawned, stretched and peered out through one of the numerous loopholes which were his pride and joy.

All was well, he noted contentedly. The oil depletion allowance was pumping efficiently. The little tungsten mine was depleting nicely. And out front, no shoots of corn marred the surface of his carefully-untended soil bank.

"I'll have to remember to not plant alfalfa next year instead of not planting corn again," mused Very. "Crop rotation is basic in modern farming."

So, whistling happily, Very sat down at the breakfast table with a cup of coffee and the books of the Very Foundation.

For, like all middle-class Americans in the year 1976, Very had created a tax-free foundation to which he contributed all his assets and earnings. In turn, it paid him a generous tax-free expense account on which to live.

He was just checking the prices of his tax-free municipal bonds when he was interrupted by his wife, Vivian, an attractive, graying non-profit corporation.

"That snooty Mrs. Van der Hovey cut me dead at the Tax Deductible Charity Ball last night," she said, her lips quivering.

"Who do they think they are?" Very said angrily. "Their foundations may be larger than my foundation, but I don't pay a penny in taxes either."

She claims her family's been tax-free for three generations," said Mrs. Very.

"And that reminds me, you'd better speak to your daughter, Verona. She's been seeing that trashy Grommet boy again."

"He's not trashy!" cried Verona. "His family may be poor and pay taxes, but it's not his fault."

"Blood will out," said Mrs. Very ominously. "He'll grow up a tax-paying wastrel. You'll see."

"It's not fair," said Verona with the rebellion of youth. "The Grommets pay taxes because they're poor and they're poor because they pay taxes. There's no way out for them."

"The poor will always be with us, dear, and so will taxes," said Very in fatherly fashion as he leafed through the morning mail. "After all, somebody has to pay them. What's this!"

He stared at the envelope. "Internal Revenue Service." With trembling fingers he tore it open. "Good Lord!" he cried. "I miscalculated the straight-line depreciation allowance on my 1948 Webley-Vickers tuning fork. I owe them a dollar-sixty-eight!"

"It won't break you, Dad," said Verona with a shrug.

"Oh, you don't understand," sobbed her mother. "We'll never be able to hold up our heads again—not once word gets around that we are (she shuddered uncontrollably) taxpayers!"

"Well, I think it's high time the Government caught up with you and your silly Very Foundation," said Verona with a sniff. "It's nothing but a crooked, unfair tax dodge."

"It may be a tax dodge to you, young lady, but to me it's all that its full name implies," said her father with dignity, "The Very Foundation of America."

The Rich Are Always With Us

No one is more pleased with Mr. Nixon's bold new poverty program than that veteran poverty fighter, Jud Joad, who's been fighting poverty man and boy for nigh on to 60 years.

"Just think, Maude," he told his wife as they sat rocking on the porch of their little cabin near Appalachia Corners, "we'll get $1600 a year. And we can keep half what I make over that, if'n I ca· find work."

"I'll believe it when I see it," said Maude.

"But while we're counting our blessings," said Jud thoughtfully, "we ought to think of those folks less fortunate than us."

"Like who?" asked Maude with interest.

"Like Senator Eastland," said Jud. "He's going to have to tighten his belt."

"Who's he?" asked Maude.

"Why, when it comes to the dole, he's just about the biggest man in the whole country. He gets maybe $200,000 a year from the Government in welfare for not growing cotton on his plantation down Mississippi way. He's kind of an idol of mine."

"I don't see where he's got much troubles," said Maude.

"That's 'cause you don't understand the President's new program. He aims to get all us idle poor folk off the welfare and back to honest work. Now that may be dandy for you and me, but what's Senator Eastland fit for?"

"What'd you say he did, Jud?"

"He don't grow cotton. I reckon it ain't easy. You got to decide when not to plough, when not to plant, when not to spray and fertilize and chop. And just when things are looking good, along comes a good growing spell and wipes you out."

"And he makes all that money? My stars, Jud, why don't you show a little gumption and not grow cotton out back of the woodpile there?"

"I tried. But the Government man said the soil ain't fit to grow cotton so it ain't worth not growing it on. The Senator's lucky. He's got good bottom land."

"Well, Jud, maybe if'n they stop paying him for not growing cotton, he'll pull hisself together and find honest work."

"Doing what, Maude? Not growing cotton don't fit you for much. Oh, he could maybe not grow sorghum or barley, but I don't reckon there's much cash in it. Nope, I figure he'll have to go through one of them job retraining programs like Cousin Willie did."

"How's that, Jud?"

"You know, Maude, they'll relocate him up North out of that there depressed area he lives in. And maybe they'll loan him a mite to set hisself up in business. I seen his picture and he'd make a right fine restaurant owner. 'Senator Eastland's Mississippi Fried Cotton—finger-sticking good.' Or something like that."

"Fried cotton, Jud? What'd that taste like?"

"Like most Southern cooking, Maude. But you take my word, the Senator'll put up a good fight before he settles for any little $1600 a year. And rightly so. He ain't used to chick peas and lard like us."

"Now I ain't gainsaying you, Jud, but are you sure the President aims to include this here Senator Eastland in our poverty program? It just don't seem likely somehow."

"I hope you're right, Maude. It wouldn't be fitting." Jud scratched his chin reflectively. "And like I've always said, this here country's big enough for two poverty programs—one for the rich and one for the poor."

The War on Affluence

The Richard M. Nixon Welfare Plan is receiving kudos everywhere for its ambitious and charitable goal of helping the poor lead useful, productive lives.

And it certainly sounds like half the answer to America's domestic ills.

The other half is, of course, The V. Thomas Sullivan Welfare Plan. Its ambitious and charitable goal is to help the rich lead useful, productive lives.

For far too long, this Nation has paid little heed to the problems of the rich. For generations these forgotten Americans have been trapped in a vicious cycle of wealth.

In rich white ghettoes from Palm Beach to Palm Springs, they breed untrammeled. Their children grow up in this subculture understanding little and caring less about the middle-class American values—such as thrift, ambition and the virtues of honest toil.

Unskilled, untrained, untutored in the ethic that made this country great, is it any wonder that most lead lives of indolence, drunkenness and sloth? Yet, as their numbers swell, how long can we support these burdens on our society?

Already resentment is growing. "I worked for mine," grumbles a Peoria, Ill., pizza maker. "Why can't they?"

Before it is too late, warns the noted sociologist, V. Thomas Sullivan, the Government must take bold steps to integrate the rich into our society. He envisions a full-scale War on Affluence with maximum feasible participation by the rich.

The first step must be to somehow overcome the inherent suspicion of these ghetto dwellers toward outsiders. Anyone who has penetrated Palm Beach or Palm Springs knows how deeply ingrained this is.

Skilled and dedicated social workers must break down these barriers by visiting the homes of the rich, winning their trust and confidence, and showing them how to lead better lives.

There is no reason that rich women cannot be taught to cook simple, nutritious meals, clean their own houses and sew their own basic clothes. Family Service Agencies could provide counseling to reduce the high incidence of broken homes and alcoholism in these ghettoes.

For the children, a massive Headstart Program, leaning heavily on Horatio Alger stories, is envisioned with busing later to middle-class schools so that they may be inculcated with middle-class values.

Admittedly, the rich father poses a problem. Unskilled workers are a drug on the labor market. Only through massive vocational training, with Job Corps Centers in the heart of every ghetto, can we hope to fit them for honest employment.

But basically what is needed is an economic incentive to work. As long as the rich are given more money for sitting around the house, they will continue to lead idle and dissolute lives. And thus new laws allowing them to keep half what they earn over a minimum of, say, $1600 a year seem only logical.

Understandably, some social bigots contend the only reason the rich don't work is that they are inherently lazy. However, tolerance dictates that we give them not charity, but a chance—the opportunity, training and incentive to get a job.

For hard work, as Mr. Nixon points out, builds character and promotes happiness. And in this great democracy of ours, what's good enough for the poor is certainly good enough for the rich.

Happy Days Are Here Again

Now that Mr. Nixon has produced his first budget, the experts are analyzing his economic policies. And it's becoming increasingly clear that he's embarked on a bold and courageous course to cure the Nation's ills.

In one fell swoop, Mr. Nixon hopes to lick the worries that most plague the average American—high prices, high taxes, pollution, overpopulation, the draft, urban sprawl and the weird conduct of our young.

It should be obvious to all by now that the President has brilliantly conceived and is daringly pushing forward the only possible solution to all these problems: another depression.

No one is happier with this turn of events than that little band of militant do-gooders called "The League to Bring Back the Depression."

For years, the League, whose motto is "Two Chickens in Every Garage," has been hopelessly bucking a rising tide of prosperity. But at a League rally the other night, victory was in the air.

"The Depression," Chairman Grufney Grommet told a wildly-cheering throng of middle-aged matrons and businessmen, "is just around the corner!"

"Yes, sir, look at the stock market," cried a balding banker elatedly. "Why it's '29 all over again."

"And unemployment's up again," said a portly manufacturer. "Pretty soon I'll be able to hang out a help wanted sign and a hundred men will line up, hats in hand."

"Just think," said a housewife, a nostalgic lump in her throat, "bread for ten cents a loaf, a first-run movie for a quarter."

"And don't forget taxes," said an elderly accountant. "Why in 1931 the whole national budget was only $3.5 billion. A man got to keep what he earned."

"We're overlooking the broad picture," said a sociologist. "Among the other benefits that will accrue are the elimination of the two-car family and a drastic decline in the birth rate—thus reducing smog and overpopulation by at least an X factor."

"And no draft," said a mother excitedly. "Imagine having an Army of only 134,000 men again—all volunteers."

"As soon as we can no longer afford disposable bottles and throw-away plastic containers," said an engineer, "the garbage problem will be eliminated."

A bearded psychologist spoke up. "Best of all, a depression will close the generation gap," he said.

"Instead of making revolutions, the young will be concerned solely, as we were, with making good."

"There's one problem a depression won't lick," said a crotchety gentleman in the rear. "And that's poverty."

"Perhaps not," said Chairman Grommet with a smile. "But at least the poor will no longer feel alone."

A motion to commend Mr. Nixon as "the greatest President since Herbert Hoover" caused spirited debate.

While all agreed with the sentiment, some felt an endorsement by the League wouldn't be favorably received by the White House. In fact, a few argued that it could scuttle Mr. Nixon's entire economic program.

"Nonsense," said Chairman Grommet. "Nothing can stop an idea whose time has come."

So the motion was adopted. The meeting adjourned with a rousing rendition of "Happy Days Are Almost Here Again." There wasn't a dry eye in the house.

Man's Worst Enemy

Once upon a time there was no one to stop people from hitting other people over the head. Or stealing their goods. Or enslaving their fellow men. It was terrible.

Naturally, the people who got hit, robbed or enslaved didn't care much for this. So they formed a self-protection association. They called it a "Government."

"The prime function of the Government," they agreed, "is to protect each of us from others and thus insure our freedom."

So the Government hired policemen and soldiers to hit people over the head who hit people over the head. Which helped put a stop to that.

Of course, other people formed Governments, too. And the people of one Government marched off to hit people of other Governments over the head and steal their goods and enslave them. So people needed Governments even more in order to protect them from other Governments.

So Governments grew bigger. Because the biggest Government could protect its people best.

Understandably, bigger Governments needed more money. So they took it away from the people under the threat of force.

"This isn't stealing," explained the Government. "This is taxes."

And as armies grew bigger, the Government took away the people's sons under threat of force and trained them to be killers.

"This isn't slavery," explained the Government. "This is patriotism."

But it was all done to protect each individual from others. And no one could complain about that.

Even after the Government had done all it could to protect each man from others, it still wanted to do more. So it brought forth a brave new concept: it would henceforth protect each man from himself, too.

It said each man was too short-sighted to save money for his old age. So it forced him to do so and called it "Social Security."

It said each man was too careless to lay aside money for his taxes. So it forced him to do so and called it "Withholding."

For his own good, it told him which books he could read and which movies he could see. It told him whom he could make love to and how. It told him he could smoke only the dried vegetable that produced lung cancer and not that which produced euphoria—all for his own good.

Solely to protect him from himself, it made him wear a seat belt when he drove a car and a helmet when he rode a motorcycle.

And from there it was but an easy step to force each man to budget his money, his time and his energy in Government-approved fashion.

So each man arose every morning at the hour the Government thought best for him, did his prescribed calisthenics, performed his approved daily chores, consumed his properly-balanced dinner, read his required reading and went to bed when the Government told him to—all, of course, solely for his own good.

Thus each man was not only protected from others, but from his own carelessness, laziness and wantonness. And each man thereby led a far more healthy, secure and constructive life.

It was terrible.

Moral: If man has to be protected from himself, he isn't worth the bother.

Let Them Eat Winstons

Congress, which worries constantly about our health, is budgeting $2.6 million this year for nagging us into quitting smoking.

Of course, Congress also worries about the health of the tobacco industry. So it's spending $73.2 million this year to promote smoking.

The lion's share of this, $31.3 million, goes to buy up surplus tobacco which we ship to poor, starving people abroad under our Food for Peace Program.

Including $31.3 million worth of tobacco in our Food for Peace packages may seem heartless to some.

There, for example, is a spindly African native tottering down the jungle trail in the last stages of starvation. He stumbles on a package labeled: "U.S. Food for Peace." With trembling fingers, he tears it open. Inside, is a carton of Winstons. With dimming eyes, he reads the legend: "Winstons taste good—like a cigarette should."

So he eats them.

Naturally, eating cigarettes is not going to help our starving friends abroad. Nor, if they don't get hooked on cigarettes, is it going to help our tobacco farmers.

What is obviously needed is a vigorous technical aid program to teach the underprivileged, backward peoples of the world to smoke:

"No, sir, you light the other end. That's it. Now suck in the smoke. There, there. Let me hit you on the back a couple of times. Fine. In a couple of days, you'll learn to love it."

Once we have our poverty-stricken friends overseas hooked, think of the humanitarian satisfaction we'll garner, shipping them packages of tobacoo to ease their cravings. Think of the pleasure they'll enjoy, lighting up that first, glorious, after-breakfast cigarette. If they had any breakfast.

But our program is not merely humanitarian, it's ecologically sound. Congress is spending not only $31.3 million on Tobacco for Peace, but $27.9 million on tobacco export subsidies and $240,000 for cigarette advertising abroad.

Thus we see that Congress in its wisdom is appropriating $2.6 million to get Americans to smoke less and $59.4 million to get foreigners to smoke more.

The goal of Congress is clear: a thriving tobacco export trade run by non-smoking, healthy Americans, all happily singing, "Oh, you can ship Salems out of the country, but . . ."

Such a program will not only save the economy, it will save the world. For we are faced with a population explosion. And many an expert warns that we simply must stop sending food abroad to starving people. For their own good.

What better substitute than tobacco? What better product to snuff out overpopulation? How good it is to know that our friends abroad will die happy.

For there is no confirmed cigarette smoker alive today who doesn't believe in his heart of hearts in that ringing slogan:

"I'd rather smoke than live."

For Sale: One Used Government

Herewith another unwritten chapter from that unpublished text, "A History of the World, 1950 to 1999." Its title: "Government Can Pay."

Mr. Nixon's decision to turn the U.S. Post Office over to a corporation proved wise. By 1972, for the first time in a century, the postal system was in the black.

The Administration was elated. "If the Post Office can pay, so can other agencies of Government," said Mr. Nixon in a televised address. "All that is required is to eliminate inefficient Government bureaucrats and let private initiative take over the job."

The next day he announced the sale of the Defense Department to the Military-Industrial Complex, Ltd.

A Complex spokesman projected an earnings rate of 8.3 per cent on the marketing of surplus weapons, the leasing of troops to foreign dictators under the "Rent-an-Army" plan, and the sale of Army-Navy game tickets.

The Rent-an-Army Plan—under the slogan, "What Price Glory?"—caused initial controversy. But it was pointed out that it would mean little change in U.S. foreign policy, except to make wars once again profitable.

Patriots complained that sale of the Defense Department would leave the country defenseless. But the Complex pledged it would stand ready to defend the U.S. at all costs (on a cost-plus contract) against any lower bidder.

More outcries were raised the following week on the sale of the Internal Revenue Service to the Mafia. But this proved the most efficient move of all.

Mafia agents simply called on each taxpayer and asked two questions. "What was your take?" and "Where's our cut?"

Tax collections soared. The number of delinquent taxpayers fell to zero. And most Americans agreed that a visit from the Mafia sure beat filling in all those tax forms.

With these successes behind him, Mr. Nixon moved swiftly. In a package deal, Disney Enterprises purchased NASA and Congress for conversion into Spaceland and Historyland, respectively.

The AFL-CIO bought Labor and the Grange bought Agriculture, though both complained that they had, in effect, long owned both departments already.

The State Department was sold to a conglomerate of travel agencies and catering services, which could well employ its expertise. But there were no takers, unfortunately, for the Commerce Department—no one being able to figure out what it did.

Mr. Nixon's only major setback was over Health, Education and Welfare. "We must put this Nation's welfare programs on a paying basis," he warned grimly.

But no way was ever found. Thus, in keeping with sound business practices, the welfare program was declared bankrupt and the poor were paid off at the rate of ten cents on the dollar.

There was some talk that Mr. Nixon planned to sell everything in sight. He heatedly denied it. "I did not become President," he said, "to preside over the liquidation of the American Government." And he pledged to keep forever one U.S. agency—the Mint.

And thus it was that the Nixon Administration achieved its unvoiced goal: a Government that did nothing but make money.

On The Death of Robert Kennedy

The anger grew. As the tiny figures swirled and eddied across the television screen and told their conflicting stories in shock and horror, the anger grew.

That this should happen once again to the Kennedys. That this should happen once again to all of us.

It was an all-encompassing anger. It encompassed the sickness of our society, the unfairness of life, the callousness of God.

"I did it for my country," a news announcer quoted the gunman as saying. "I did it because I love my country."

Suddenly the anger focused. It focused not so much on the gunman as on all those like him among us—those who know what is good for the rest of us, those who push and shove and trample and shoot and kill in the righteousness of their own glorious cause.

Save us, dear Lord, from those who would save us.

For no man consciously does evil. Each man must justify to himself what he does. And how easy that is for those who know they serve in a righteous cause.

How easy for the assassin to pull the trigger, for he knows what's good for his country. How easy for the Nazi to strangle a Jew, for he knows he builds a Reich that will last a thousand years. How easy for a Communist to purge a dissenter, for he knows he creates a brave new world.

How easy it is for the Christian or the Moslem to butcher his fellow man, for he is the repository of divine truth. How easy for the Viet Cong terrorist or the Saigon police chief, for each knows he kills to save his nation.

How easy for the Klansman to lynch a nigger, for he knows he saves the Southern Way of Life. How easy for a Black militant to cry, "Burn, baby, burn," for he knows this will make his people free.

How easy for the radical left to strive to tear down this sorry scheme of things entire, for they know our society is destroying our souls. How easy for the radical right to form secret guerrilla bands, trained to shoot and kill, for they know they must save us all.

How easy it is. How easy it is for the righteous to justify what they do.

So the anger grew. And with it the hatred. I hated. We must somehow save ourselves from these hateful people who would march militantly over us to save our society, our nation, our world.

In my own self-righteousness, I hated more than I can remember ever hating before. In my own self-righteousness, I could gladly have seen them all destroyed. In my own self-righteousness.

And now, in reflection, I am more convinced than ever in what I have long believed:

If I would remake the world, I had better start with me.

8

The War

And All That

The Americanization of America

It was in the 43rd year of our lightning campaign to wipe the dread Viet-Narian guerrillas out of West Vhtnnng.

The Vice President of Vhtnnng, Whar Dat Ky, who had long plotted to seize the executive washroom, decided to pay a two-week visit to America.

Wherever he went in the United States, Vice President Ky was greeted warmly, in fact hotly, with rocks, jeers, bricks, catcalls, eggs, boos and rotten rutabagas.

By the time he managed to limp home, Ky was understandably concerned.

"I see you got stoned again," said his suspicious Premier, General Hoo Dat Opp Dar.

"Hoo, boy, have we got troubles," said Ky. "Everywhere in America rocks and bricks are flying all over the place. The whole country, obviously, is about to go down the tube."

"Who cares?" said the Foreign Minister, General Hoo Khars, with a shrug.

"How would you like to run our dumb little country on $30 billion less a year?" said Ky grimly.

The American President was initially surprised to receive an offer of 4000 Vhtnnngian military advisors to the National Guard.

But as the long-time Vhtnnngian Ambassador to Washington Won Ngo Bac, explained: "Your country, Mr. President, is being torn apart by veteran Communist radicals. When it comes to wiping out Vet-Com terrorists, our troops have 43 years experience."

It made sense. The first contingent of Vhtnnngian advisors arrived at Kent State in June of 1972.

Naturally, some Americans were outraged at being shot at by foreign troops and many moderates went over to the side of the Vet-Com. The war escalated.

"I will never send Asian boys to fight a war American boys should fight themselves," vowed General Hoo Dat Don Dar.

But what could he do? With American troops scattered all over the world, Washington was losing ground to the Vet-Com. Vhtnnng was losing face.

By May of 1973, there were 500,000 Vhtnnngian combat troops in the U.S. The Loyal Royal Air Force was bombing the H. Rap Brown Trail from the Mexican marijuana fields daily and had long since defoliated California.

Vhtnnngian troops staged a huge sweep through Canada to destroy "the privileged sanctuaries" of draft dodgers and other Vet-Com troublemakers. And though the Vet-Com Pentagon was never found, the operation was declared "a tremendous success."

It was at this point that a young pacifist, Duc Quik, heaved a brick through a window in the capital of Sag On, crying, "Down with Vhtnnngian imperialism!" In a week, the last Vhtnnngian troop had been withdrawn from American soil.

"We have decided that the best way to end the American War," explained General Hoo Dat Don Dar calmly, "is to Americanize it. Have a nice time fighting among yourselves."

While most Americans weren't sorry to see the Vhtnnngians leave their smoldering, denuded country, they were somewhat surprised by the speed of the operation.

"Why prolong the agony?" said General Hoo. "We've seen how dissension over a foreign war can tear a nation apart. It isn't worth it."

"Do you mean," demanded our President angrily, "that preserving the present American Government isn't worth the troubles you'd face at home?"

"Heck," said General Hoo, "it isn't even worth $30 billion a year."

Seven Days in Anytime

THURSDAY—A Pentagon spokesman today confirmed reports that "a small, tactical nuclear device" had been dropped on Red China Tuesday.

He said it may have inflicted "some casualties" on a "little village in remote Sinkiang Province." He said "one or more" American planes were involved.

There was no protest from Peking. Peking Radio has been silent for the past 48 hours.

FRIDAY—Secretary of Defense Laird told the Senate Foreign Relations Committee that Chinese casualties "might be somewhat higher than at first anticipated."

He denied, however, that it was an American bombing attack. It was, he said, "an advance retaliatory protective mission" aimed at "saving American lives in Southeast Asia."

The mission was necessary, he said, to prevent Chinese anti-aircraft batteries from firing on unarmed American reconnaisance planes attempting to assess the damage.

SATURDAY—President Nixon was said to have told four Republican women from Dubuque at a private White House garden reception that they need "no longer worry" about Red China. "It has ceased to exist," they quoted him as saying.

The Pentagon would say only that it was "revising its casualty estimates." One source, however, said, "It won't go any higher than 500 million at most."

SUNDAY—Appearing on Face the Press, Senator Fulbright accused Secretary Laird of having lied to the Foreign Relations Committee. Instead of "one small device," he said, "we rained more than a thousand megatons of nuclear bombs on every corner of China."

Secretary Laird immediately called a press conference to deny he had lied. "Senator Fulbright," he said, "didn't ask the right questions."

At the same time, Laird said radioactive fallout from the mission "poses no danger at this time, except to localized areas of the Western Pacific."

MONDAY—Evacuation of American troops and officals from Vietnam and other Asian areas began this morning. The Pentagon described the move as "precautionary" in view of "a small radioactive cloud in the area."

TUESDAY—The White House said The Cloud was now centered over Guam but "should dissipate within a very few hours." A spokesman said U.S. regrets for any inconvenience The Cloud may have caused had been cabled to American allies in the Far East. No replies have yet been received.

WEDNESDAY—In a televised address tonight, President Nixon said there was "no cause for alarm." At the same time, he paid tribute to "our brave fellow Americans" in the Western United States.

"They were part of our cherished national heritage," he said, "and both Pat and I shall deeply miss them."

THURSDAY—The President, broadcasting from Air Force One at 50,000 feet, said "the short-lived crisis" was definitely over. The Cloud, he said, was now moving out over the Atlantic.

"I know I shall be criticized for having done what was right, as I have been in the past," he said. "But never before have we been given a greater opportunity to build a better and stronger America.

"Each of us, in my opinion, has been given a fresh start. And that goes, rightly or wrongly, for every living American down there below me tonight."

Unfortunately, there weren't any.

Private Drab Finds the Enemy

The U.S. Command has ordered American forces to search out marijuana fields in South Vietnam and turn them over to South Vietnamese troops for burning. The idea is to cut down the growing use of pot by GIs.—News Item

Baker Company squatted on a hillside staring morosely at the smoke wafting gently from the fields below toward the far end of the valley.

"Congratulations, men" said Captain Buck Ace, holstering his pearl-handled .45. "This has been one of the most successful search-and-destroy missions in regimental annals. Another five acres wiped out to the last plant."

None of the men stirred. They simply squatted there silent, motionless, shoulders slumped, staring.

"What's the matter men? said the Captain irritably. "You ought to be waving your helmets and cheering. You there, Drab, speak up."

"It just don't seem fair, sir," said Private Oliver Drab, 378-18-4454, gloomily. "I wish it was rice."

"Rice? What are you talking about Drab?"

"Well, sir, I can see how come we destroy their rice fields. Some of it, they grow for the enemy. But that stuff down there, they grow it for us."

Captain Ace smiled and put his hand on Private Drab's shoulder. "Look, son," he said, "that's marijuana down there. It's bad for you. It makes you euphoric. That means it blurs your mind so you don't recognize the seriousness of the problems you face."

Drab nodded solemnly. "Yes, sir, it sure is a comfort and a blessing."

The Captain frowned. "Look, soldier, anything that impairs the efficiency of the American fighting man has got to be destroyed." He relented a bit. "Come on, men, let's move out. Maybe when we get back to base, we can find ourselves a couple of beers apiece."

"And destroy them, sir?" asked Private Drab worriedly.

Captain Ace laughed. "Nobody's got anything against a soldier having a couple of beers after a hard day's work. Maybe even getting a little drunk. That's a soldier's life, eh, men?"

"Yes, sir," agreed Private Drab, "But I still don't see the difference between beer and pot."

The Captain's patience snapped. "Damn it, I'll tell you in four words, Drab. Thirty days hard labor. Now move out."

Private Drab sighed. "Yes, sir. But could we maybe circle around the far end of the valley?"

"Now where in hell will that get us?"

"Downwind, sir," said Private Drab brightly.

Later, as they slogged along, Private Drab said to his friend Corporal Partz, "Big deal, destroying that pot. It's just going to drive the price up."

"Every time I look around this lousy country," said Corporal Partz, "I'm for destroying all I can."

"You are? Honest?"

"Yep," said Corporal Partz, spitting thoughtfully. "One joint at a time."

The Best Way To Kill People

Scene: The Heavenly Real Estate Office. The Landlord is seated behind his desk, working on a plan for developing a new galaxy, as his collection agent, Gabriel, enters.

The Landlord: Hmmm, a billion bushels of starshine, an aura of moonglow, ten parsecs of . . . What is it, Gabriel?

Gabriel: It's that little blue-green jewel of a planet you love so, sir. The inhabitants are arguing over how best to kill each other.

The Landlord: They're what?

Gabriel: The leaders are finally meeting to talk about throwing their nuclear weapons in the sea. They are afraid they will kill each other too fast with nuclear weapons. And one leader, praise you, has even ordered his stockpiles of poison gas destroyed because killing people with poison gas is inhumane.

The Landlord: By me, that's wonderful! They're making progress.

Gabriel: Best of all, some soldiers who lined up and killed several hundred women and children and old men will be tried to show the world that rifle bullets are the worst way to kill women and children.

The Landlord: The worst way?

Gabriel: Yes, sir. The best way, it's generally agreed, is to kill them with bombs, rockets, artillery shells and napalm. Those who kill women and children in these ways are called heroes and given every honor.

The Landlord (frowning): I'm not sure I . . .

Gabriel: I think it's a distance factor, sir. To kill women and children at less than 500 paces is an atrocity; at more than 500 paces, it's an act of heroism.

The Landlord: Hmmm. But why did these soldiers shoot these women and children?

Gabriel: Almost everybody blames it on the war, sir. Most of the soldiers were forced to go fight in this terrible war when they didn't want to. And the frustrations of fighting in a terrible war, everybody agrees, drove them half crazy.

The Landlord (shaking his head): Poor soldiers. But at least most of the people in the soldiers' country are against this terrible war that drives soldiers half crazy.

Gabriel: No, sir. Most of them are for it. They wish to continue sending their soldiers to be driven half crazy in this terrible war. Even those who are against it contribute money for bullets and bombs and rockets and shells and napalm.

The Landlord: Why, then, they're accomplices. When will they be tried?

Gabriel: No, sir, they're called patriots. Those few who refuse to contribute to killing women and children are called traitors.

The Landlord: Hmmm. And what will happen to these soldiers if they are convicted of the horrible atrocity of lining up human beings and shooting them?

Gabriel: Oh, they'll be lined up and shot. Either that or they'll be placed in a chamber and killed with poison gas. Everyone agrees that's the most humane way to kill people.

The Landlord (confused): But you said . . . Well, then, if poison gas is the most humane, it's obviously the best way to kill women and children. There's your answer, Gabriel.

Gabriel: They don't think so, sir. You see, some frightful people called Nazis once killed millions of women and children that way. And now it's considered an atrocious atrocity to kill more than two people at a time with poison gas. (after a long silence) Do you want to give them any advice, sir?

The Landlord: By me in heaven, yes! There's clearly but one simple, rational solution. Tell them, Gabriel, flatly and succinctly: "Thou shalt not kill!"

Gabriel: Excuse me, sir, but you already told them that

a millenium or so ago.

The Landlord (with a sigh): So I did. You know, Gabriel, it's a shame it never caught on down there.

The Fix Is On in West Vhtnnng

It was in the 43rd year of our lightning campaign to drive the dread Viet Narian guerrillas out of West Vhtnnng. The President's Secret Plan to End the War was working wonders.

The President's Machiavellian strategy called for slowly, inexorably withdrawing American troops from West Vhtnnng until Communist East Vhtnnng threw in the sponge. At first, the sheer brilliance of these tactics blinded the enemy.

"Let's see, they're going to withdraw their troops until we surrender?" said East Vhtnnng Premier Nho Diem Ghud, scratching his head. "These occidentals are sure inscrutable."

"They must know something we don't know," muttered General Wyn Na Phieu, the famed tactician. "Obviously, we must counter by out-withdrawing them, thus forcing them to surrender first."

"No, no," cried Foreign Minister Ngo Mahn Ngo, who had once studied football at Rutgers and was considered an expert on American mental processes. "They are simply trying to save face. We must capitalize on this American peculiarity. Now, listen to my Secret Plan to End the War . . ."

The first indication that the enemy was up to something came when General Wyn Na Phieu was replaced as battlefield commander by General Lhu Sa Phieu.

The following day, new enemy orders were captured, and security precautions were trebled at every B-girl bar in West Vhtnnng. The captured orders from General Lhu Sa Phieu to his troops read: "Take a dive."

That afternoon, two privates of the Loyal Royal West Vhtnnng Army, happily playing phing-phong (the local version of whist), were surprised by a division of dread Viet Narian guerrillas.

"Ai-yee" cried the Viet Narians. "It is the awesome Loyal Royal Army!" And they fled.

Such incidents multiplied. The Loyal Royal Army was so encouraged that it actually got up out of its trenches and charged. This way and that. In quick order, it captured such "major enemy strongholds" as Cao Dung, Whar Dat and Hoo Kars.

Indeed, every time the Americans withdrew another 50,000 troops, the Loyal Royal Army scored another victory.

"My Secret Plan to End the War is working just as I predicted!" cried an elated President. And then he added with a frown: "I just wish I knew why."

But the pace of withdrawals was stepped up and on July 4th the last of America's 500,000 troops embarked for home—leaving the Loyal Royal Army, as the President put it, "to win or lose this war on their own."

They lost it, of course, the very next day.

But most Vhtnnngians were happy not to be bombed or shot any more. And most Americans were happy not to have to cough up $30 billion a year for a dumb war nobody liked. And the President was happy that his Secret Plan had worked.

"I said I'd never be the first American President to lose a war and I'm not," he said proudly. "The Loyal Royal Army lost it all by themselves."

The victors gave full credit to Ngo Mahn Ngo. But he was modest. "I was able to understand the President's Secret Plan," he said humbly, "because of what I learned in college in America."

And he skillfully rolled himself another marijuana cigarette.

Hawks and Doves

The Dove idly swirled his sherry and stared out the restaurant window at the busy streets of the capital below.

"I know, I know," he said, irritably brushing his longish, greying hair behind his ear with the palm of his hand. "But how can we be sure this anti-ballistic missile system of ours would work?"

"Frankly, we can't," admitted the Hawk, a square-jawed general, his broad chest covered with battle ribbons. "But they can't be sure either. And hopefully, that may be enough to deter them from launching a first strike against us."

"Oh, come now," said the Dove. "I can't believe all this talk that they're developing a first-strike capability. Surely, they're as afraid of a nuclear war as we are."

"Their people, maybe. But do you really trust their leaders? We've seen them march into one country after another to prop up their puppet regimes. Never forget that they've vowed to destroy us."

The Dove looked uneasy. "But they'd never risk a nuclear war," he said. "What makes you think they're planning to strike first?"

The Hawk leaned forward in his chair. "They've openly admitted that they're targeting their missiles, not on our cities, but on our missile installations."

The Dove relaxed and smiled. "Well, I'd certainly rather they blew up our missiles than our cities."

"Not if you think it through," said the Hawk grimly. "If they were really concerned with our striking first, why target on our missile installations? If we fired first, our silos would be empty. The only conceivable reason is that they are planning on wiping out our missiles in a surprise attack. They could then destroy our defenseless cities at will."

The Dove frowned. "But surely . . ."

"Another thing," said the Hawk. "They admit they're constantly improving the accuracy of their missiles. They claim they can now hit within 400 yards of their target. There's no point in such accuracy if you're aiming at a city. It would only be valuable in a first strike against our missile installations."

"I can't believe . . ."

"They admit they already have enough land and undersea-based missiles to inflict unacceptable damage on us in a second strike. And yet they are constantly building more. Why? They seek our total annihilation."

"You make them sound like madmen."

"They may well be. Why else would they be developing diseases for which there's no cure and nerve gases for which there's no defense? Why else would they be working on multiple warheads to treble the existing nuclear terror?"

"Perhaps in the upcoming disarmament talks . . ."

"You know they're stalling about opening disarmament negotiations. They've as much as admitted it. Why? I tell you, we've no choice but to step up our missile building program. We must maintain nuclear parity no matter what the cost, or face extinction."

The Dove sighed. "It will mean curtailing our domestic programs in order to maintain a balance of terror," he said. "But I suppose you are right. You can count on my support."

He stared moodily out the window for a moment at a Russian family happily crossing Red Square.

"Tell me this, General Zhukov," he said, shaking his head. "Why can't these American madmen be more like us?"

Support Our Boy In Vietnam

Washington, Sept. 12, 1972

Waves of B-52s and carrier based bombers hit Communist supply routes today in North Vietnam, Cambodia, Laos, Thailand, Burma and Tibet.

"I have ordered this all-out assault," the President grimly told a national television audience, "in order to protect our troop in Vietnam."

The name of our troop in Vietnam is, of course, Private Oliver Drab, 378-18-4454. He has become something of a cause celebre since the last of his fellow GIs were withdrawn six weeks ago.

The President justified today's attack by citing his policy declaration of February 17, 1971: "As far as our air power is concerned, it will be directed against those military activities which I determine are directed against and thereby threaten our remaining forces in South Vietnam."

He said recent Communist build-ups on the Ho Chi Minh and other trails certainly threatened Private Drab. "I will not hesitate to fully unleash American air power in Asia," said the President firmly, "as long as the safety of one American boy is at stake."

At the same time, the controversy over keeping Private Drab in Vietnam continued to grow.

A near riot broke out yesterday at the Washington Monument when Peace groups staged a huge rally under the slogan: "Bring Our Boy Home!" They were confronted by several hundred hard-hat construction workers carrying placards declaring: "Support Our Fighting Man in Vietnam!"

In the resulting melee, seven pacifists were badly bruised and five hard hats severely dented.

Despite public protest, however, it appeared unlikely that Private Drab would be withdrawn in the forseeable future. For one thing, the Saigon government is unalterably opposed to such a move.

"Words cannot express how highly we value the fighting qualities of our beloved American ally," Vice President Ky told newsmen while holding his hand over his heart," "and all those big beautiful bombers that come with him."

For another, with Private Drab at his post, efforts in Congress to curtail the President's power to launch ever-expanding air attacks in Asia have been stymied—no Congressman being willing to vote for a measure that might jeopardize a single American life.

Meanwhile, a group of 14 Republican Congressmen, headed by Representative B. J. Broadbinder, arrived in Vietnam to "assess the morale and needs of our boy in the front lines." They visited Drab in his foxhole 47 miles northwest of Saigon.

"When it comes to the President's withdrawal program," said Broadbinder, clapping the Private on the shoulder, "you are living testimonial to its success."

"Yes, sir," said Private Drab, nodding. "I hope to keep it that way."

Broadbinder frowned. "I trust you realize, Private," he said, "that you are the most heavily protected soldier in military history. At this very moment, thousands of American bombers are blasting hell out of the enemy all over Asia—just for you. Thanks to the President, you're safer than you would be at home in your own bed. I hope you appreciate the honor."

"What I'd appreciate more, sir," said Private Drab earnestly, "is the choice."

The Scapegoat That Got Away

Once upon a time there was a country called Wonderfuland that was the most wonderful country in the world. Its ideas were noble, its motives pure and it was the hope of mankind.

But one day, out of basically noble motives, Wonderfuland got bogged down in a dirty little war far, far away. As it dragged on, few people in Wonderfuland felt very good about it. While they hated to talk about it, they suspected that atrocities were being committed by both sides. And so their frustration and guilt grew.

Now since the dawn of time, men in such situations had selected scapegoats on which to heap their sins. Then, when the scapegoat was sacrificed, it would carry their sins with it—thus cleansing their guilt and refreshing their souls.

So when a young lieutenant was caught committing an atrocity, it seemed Wonderfuland at last had the scapegoat it needed.

He was not too tall, not too bright, not too sensitive, not too articulate and thoroughly guilty. In fact, he went around saying things like lining up and shooting women and babies was "no big deal."

All in all, he seemed an ideal scapegoat whose sacrifice would rid the people of their guilt. So he was tried and convicted. But an odd thing happened.

The people did not, as is customary, point at the scapegoat, cry, "There's the guilty one, not I," and breathe a sigh of relief. Instead, they made him a national hero.

No one denied his guilt, but they made up all sorts of excuses for him. No one had told him not to kill women and babies, they said. Or a higher-up had ordered him to kill women and babies, they said. And anyway, they said, what's so wrong about killing women and babies? Everyone, they said, kills women and babies in a war. And moreover . . .

Before you knew it, a song glorifying the young lieutenant had sold a million records. Before you knew it, the young lieutenant received $100,000 for his memoirs. Before you knew it, the President, himself, told the people not to worry, he would save the young lieutenant in the end.

The problem, of course, was that those who hated the war most had to blame the war, not the young lieutenant. While those who patriotically supported the war had to say that the soldiers of Wonderfuland would never do anything wrong. So the country was ironically united at last.

In the end, naturally, the President, who could count votes, gave the young lieutenant a full pardon. Congress, naturally, gave him the Medal of Honor, the highest award a grateful nation could bestow. And the people, naturally, gave him countless ticker tape parades. So naturally, he was chosen as the President's running mate in the next election and carried the ticket to victory.

Of course, children emulated this new hero, playing a game called, "Kill the Gooks." Of course, the soldiers of Wonderfuland realized that atrocites were now rewarded by fame and fortune. Of course, when the enemy now lined up and shot Wonderfuland prisoners there were no complaints. Of course, the little war grew even rottener. And, of course, Wonderfuland was no longer the hope of mankind.

So it was that the young lieutenant became the first scapegoat in history to make the people feel worse.

Moral: The one thing more stupid than sacrificing a scapegoat is to glorify one on high. For, by definition, a scapegoat carries what is worst in the people wherever it goes.

The Pentagon Wins a War

By the Spring of 1971, the Army was in serious trouble with the American public. Growing revelations of corruption, graft, atrocities and battlefield reverses had sadly undermined confidence in the Army's ability to defend the nation.

At the same time, malnourishment, functional illiteracy and blight stalked the cities and rural areas. It was clear the country was losing the War on Poverty. Yet the Department of Health, Education and Welfare had little luck in weening funds from a tight-fisted Congress.

It was then that the administration had one of its rare strokes of genius. The President radically altered his proposed Government Reorganization Plan. Congress, over stiff opposition, reluctantly passed it.

So it was that the Department of Health, Education and Welfare took over the defense of the nation. And the Pentagon took over the War on Poverty.

The results of the exchange surpassed even the wildest dreams of its proponents.

The generals in the Pentagon reacted to this new challenge with the traditional Army tactic they had become so efficient over the years in employing: They marched up Capital Hill to demand more money.

"We can see the light at the end of the tunnel," General Westmoreland confidently told the happily nodding Congressmen. And he proposed three new projects:

The first was Sky Bolt. This envisioned fleets of helicopters circling over the nation's ghettos dropping packets of cash indiscriminately on the poor. The contract would be let to the Boeing Company of Seattle. The total cost was estimated at only $1.3 million.

Second was the TFX (for "Teacher Funding, Experimental"). Lockheed, with the help of technical advisers from Rolls Royce, would be granted a contract to wipe out functional illiteracy in America. The cost estimate was $1.2 million.

Lastly, there was the ambitious ABM (for "Anti-Blight Measure"). Under this proposal, a consortium of aerospace firms, headed by Penn Central Railroad executives, would be given the job of rebuilding the cities and cleaning up pollution. Estimated cost: $1.6 million.

The Congressmen, awed as always by a general's uniform, approved the proposals as usual without a dissenting vote. Out-of-work engineers and craftsmen were rehired. Work began.

In no time, money showered down on the poor. Teachers poured into the classrooms. New housing sprang up in the slums. The air grew fit to breathe, the water fit to drink.

In the first year alone, cost overruns, to no one's surprise, amounted to $63.7 billion. But Congress, as it had for a generation, passed the huge Pentagon budget without a murmur.

As always, the money had to come from somewhere. As always, it came from the budget of Health, Education and Welfare. To make ends meet, HEW had to withdraw the remaining troops in Vietnam, end draft calls and scrap all the vast thermonuclear weapons systems it could never unleash without destroying the world.

Yet, oddly enough, the nation was far more secure than ever before. Where it had been weak, divided and on the brink of chaos, it was now, with its sicknesses cured, healthy, prosperous and united. No nation dared attack it. And new nations, to the chagrin of the communists, sought to emulate its happy blend of democracy and captialism.

The whole thing proved, as a wise philosopher later said, that: "Money can, too, buy happiness. But only if you spend it in the right places."

Join the New Fun-Filled Army

To promote recruitment, the Army is projecting an all-new fun image—a 40-hour week, go-go girls, sleeping late, private rooms and a beer dispenser at the end of the hall.

Such innovations worry many Americans. "The only thing that has preserved our civilian-led democracy," rightly says my friend, Clauswitz, "is that any civilian who got mixed up with the Army in the past 200 years thoroughly loathed it."

With this in mind, it may help to publish a letter from a typical new recruit to the folks back home.

Dear Mom & Dad—Well, I got assigned to the 114th Engineering & Surfing Battalion here in Miami Beach.

We're quartered at the Eden Roc. Being new, I didn't get a room on the beach side. It's O.K., I guess, but the sun sure shines in early and I can't sleep much past 10 a.m.

Dad, I guess you figure the Army's changed a lot since your day. But we've still got top sergeants. Ours is John (Cuddles) Wayne. And, boy, is he ever picky!

Like yesterday, he caught me down on the beach in my Hawaiian-flowered swim trunks. You should've heard what he said. "Private," he says, "I respectfully suggest you slip into your attractive Sun 'n Fun beach shirt, sir. Your shoulders are getting awfully pink."

Then he's always on me about my long hair. "Private," he says, "why don't you try a little of my Passion Oil Shampoo, sir? That salt water's making your hair dry, tacky and unmanageable and it's just ruining your natural curl."

Nag, nag, nag.

The chow's O.K., I guess—if you like frogs legs and stuff

like that. But, boy, you know what they served us last night for an appetizer? Snails! I mean real snails! Half the guys couldn't touch their Chateaubriand. Cuddles swore it'd never happened again.

The 114th is a pretty good outfit, I guess. But it sure does have its weirdos. We had one guy who went around all the time picking up cigarette butts. I guess he had this thing about cigarette butts. Cuddles finally sent him to the shrink. "I didn't like to do it, gang," he told us at Happy Hour, "but that fellow was giving the outfit a bad name."

I guess you read, Mom, about these go-go girls. Well, don't you worry any about me. The one on our floor's got thick ankles. And she's always tickling me and giggling when I'm trying to watch TV. It's enough to drive you up the wall.

I'm real lucky in one thing. The beer dispenser's just outside my room. I don't much like the wine we get with dinner. Even Cuddles admits it's "a little presumptuous."

Which reminds me. I found out today the guy I replaced "went West." That means they shipped him to Palm Springs for R&R. He got a Purple Heart out of it, though, for cirrhosis of the liver.

Well, I got to go. Tonight's movie is another skin flick. We're pretty sick of them. Cuddles keeps promising us a good Walt Disney picture. But no luck yet.

Don't worry about me. Like you said, Dad, soldiers down through history have always said the same thing to themselves to keep their spirits up. I'm saying it to me right now: "In 705 days, 13 hours and 42 minutes I'll be out of this rotten, lousy, no-good Army!"

There, I feel much better.

Your Loving Son

Our Missiles Will Save Us All

"Please, tell me again Gramps, what are those big things in the holes out beyond the forest?"

"Those are our missiles, honey. They protect us from The Enemy."

"But the missiles are all rusty, Gramps, and the holes are filled with rain water."

"Don't you worry none, honey. If The Enemy attacks our cities, they will soar up into the sky and explode like the setting sun."

"Oh, how beautiful! What's a city, Gramps?"

"Well, now, honey, a city's a great big place where thousands of people live in buildings maybe even a hundred foot high. We had dozens of cities before The Time of the Troubles."

"A thousand people all in one place. My! Where did all the cities go, Gramps?"

"Most of them got burned down during The Time of the Troubles. The poor folks burned them down because they were hungry."

"But everybody's always hungry, Gramps."

"Not then, honey. Back then, most folks had more than they could eat. And more clothes than they could wear and bigger houses than they could rightly use."

"Then why didn't they give more things to the poor people so they wouldn't burn down the cities, Gramps?"

"Well, they sure would've liked to, honey. But they had to build the missiles, instead."

"But that's silly, Gramps. You can't eat missiles."

"Don't be blasphemous, girl. You're too young to understand. We had to build missiles to protect us from The Enemy. You see, The Enemy aimed to destroy our way of life."

"But the poor people . . ."

"Our missiles protected the poor folks just as well as the rich folks, fair as fair can be. And protection comes first. Now it sure doesn't make much sense to feed a hungry man only to let The Enemy destroy him, does it?"

"Well, no, I guess not, but . . ."

"First things first, honey. So we built hundreds and hundreds of missiles. You can still see them all over the countryside. And we said, 'Now The Enemy will never dare destroy our cities.' And we were right. They never did. There, now, I think this here rat's done."

"You sure speared us a fat one, Gramps."

"Now that you understand about the missiles, honey, maybe you'd like to say the blessing. Think you can?"

"Oh, yes, Gramps. Blessed be our almighty missiles. May they protect us from The Enemy forever and ever. Amen."

"That was just fine, honey. Now you go on into the cave and catch a little shut-eye. I'll stand first watch tonight."

"Yes, Gramps. But tell me first, who's The Enemy?"

"Well, now, honey, I don't rightly remember that. But don't you fret. As long as we have our missiles, we'll be safe."

"Oh, Gramps. I'm scared. They just don't look like they'd work."

"Hush, now, honey. Some things you just got to accept on faith."

Take Courage, Men, in Small Doses

The Army has flatly denied reports that it is giving our troops in Vietnam "courage pills" to instill bravery on the field of valor. And it can now be corroborated that the report is without merit.

True, an effective courage pill was developed last year by Dr. Mark Hawkins, D.V.M., a civilian researcher in the Chemical Warfare Department.

In a demonstration at the Aberdeen Proving Grounds in September, Dr. Hawkins fed a courage pill to a field mouse, which then dove head first into a tank filled with man-eating piranhas. The report noted that the mouse was able to "inflict severe damage" on several of the fish before being torn to shreds.

The demonstration was hailed at the time by top Army officers present.

"Since the dawn of history," said General Zip K. Zapp, "brilliant tactical maneuvers conceived by general staffs have been thwarted by the refusal of troops to charge impregnable positions and other such acts of cowardice. This chemical breakthrough will revolutionize the art of warfare."

Unfortunately, the only field test of the pill proved disastrous.

Selected to conduct the test was Baker Company, 1346th Infantry, Captain Buck Ace commanding. Captain Ace chose a propitious moment: The company was pinned down in a drainage ditch by an entrenched enemy force that outnumbered it 9-1.

"Take courage, men!" cried Captain Ace. "Two tablets

followed by a sip of water."

The men bravely swallowed their courage pills and the transformation was virtually instantaneous. Hunched shoulders were squared, slack jaws were firmed, and uneasy eyes shone with a new bold light.

The first overt act of valor was taken by the Company Clerk, Private First Class Albert Grossman. Removing his glasses, Private Grossman, with an air of great satisfaction, kicked Sergeant Abner Bullhead squarely in the groin.

Ignoring the melee that followed, Captain Ace shouted: "Forward, men! Ours not to reason why; ours but to do or die. Into the jaws of death! Ch-ARRR-gge!"

"Excuse me, Captain, but there's something I've always been scared to ask you," said Private Oliver Drab, 378-18-4454, tugging at his superior's sleeve. "Are you some kind of a nut or something?"

At that point, the men of Baker Company, filled with new-found courage, did, indeed, charge. Unfortunately, they charged not into the thick of the enemy fire, but in precisely the opposite direction. According to the subsequent report, some made it half way to Saigon with the intention of commandeering a ship to take them home before the courage pills wore off and they straggled back to camp, shame-faced and hangdog.

Dr. Hawkins suggested that smaller doses of the pill might produce the desired effect without the disastrous consequences.

But the General Staff voted unanimously to scrap the entire project.

"From a military point of view," as one General put it with a suppressed shudder, "courage is nothing to fool around with."

The Fine Art of Military Spending

Several taxpayers have complained lately that multi-billion-dollar Pentagon projects such as the F-111, the C-5A and the ABM just seem to grow like Topsy with no planning nor direction.

I'm delighted to assure them that this simply isn't true. From inception to completion, all such programs are carefully guided through Congress by the top-secret Pentagon Project Planning Section.

A brief history of the $49.2 billion T4-2 Project and the role played by the Planning Section may help explain how the system works.

The T4-2 project was launched in 1965 by the Section's Sergeant Mackey Velly. It appeared as a line in the Defense Appropriations Budget: "17 quarter-inch lag screws . . . 49 cents."

Unfortunately, of course, the contractor erred and instead delivered 1700 quarter-inch bolts at a cost of $342.12. Thus in 1966 Second Lieutenant Velly requested $28.14 for 1700 quarter-inch nuts. "Without nuts," he explained, "bolts are worthless."

In the 1967 budget there was an item of $14,638.12 for cadmium steel plates. "We find we have a surplus of nuts and bolts with nothing to bolt together, First Lieutenant Velly explained. "We can thus save money and build the world's first military cadmium-steel septic tank. The technological spin-off for the civilian economy should be tremendous."

In the 1968 budget, there was a request for $13.6 million to put wheels on the septic tank.

"Our Army today," explained Captain Velly, "must be a mobile army, equipped to go anywhere."

The following year, Major Velly was back to explain an item of $143.6 million to install wings and jet engines on the T4-2 Mobile Septic Tank. "This way," he explained, "it will not only serve our airborne divisions, but save billions in shipping costs by flying itself overseas."

Congress, impressed both by the idea of saving billions and by Air Force lobbyists, agreed. The tough fight came in 1970 on the key request for $208.7 million to make the T4-2 Flying Mobile Septic Tank submersible.

"Surely our fighting Navy deserves as good a septic tank as our Army and Air Force," argued Lieutenant Colonel Velly. And who could argue with that?

In 1971, a happy Colonel Velly returned to Congress to report the project now half completed at a cost of only $12.3 billion (due to overruns). So he'd need another $12.3 billion to complete it. But Congress wouldn't want to see that first $12.3 billion go down the—ha-ha—drain, would it? It wouldn't.

So it was that on a joyous day in 1978 that a proud General Velly watched as the first T4-2 Flying Mobile Submersible Septic Tank lumbered down the runway, shedding wheels, soared 18 feet into the air, plopped down in a cattle wallow, turned turtle and sank like a stone.

Asked if he were disappointed, General Velly said no, he was more concerned about an item he'd placed in next year's budget for 86 cents worth of glue, a gutta percha golf ball and two pounds of horseshoe nails.

"With luck," he confided, eyes aglow, "it'll make the greatest spaceship the world's ever seen."

The Calf Who Didn't Want to Go

Scene: A holding pen in the Republic of Cattle. A sign on a post says, "Board 374, Bureau of Meat Inspection."

Three incredibly old bulls lounge behind a table with a flag at each end. The Board Chairman, a jowly Hereford, is in the center. Flanking him are the two Board Members, a skinny old Angus with a hooked nose and an ancient Guernsey with a crumpled horn.

The secretary, an elderly Jersey cow with a large udder and sad eyes, waits placidly on the other side of the table, chewing her cud.

A young calf enters hesitantly, his ears slightly aback, his tail twitching nervously, a wary expression in his clear, wide eyes.

The Chairman (heartily): Congratulations, son. You're a fine specimen of young calfhood. The medical examiners have found you sound of fetlock, rump and brisket.

The Calf: Thank you, sir. But . . .

The Chairman: You're a credit to young cattledom. And I'm happy to say this Board has seen fit to classify you A-1 Prime.

The Calf: Thank you, sir, but . . . (blurting it out) but I don't want to go.

The Old Angus (shocked): You don't want to go! (Suspiciously) You one of these young calves that believes in vegetarianism?

The Calf: No, sir. Not exactly, but . . .

The Ancient Guernsey (sternly): Look here son. If you're claiming to be one of these conscientious objectors, you gotta prove you believe in a Sacred Cow. Can you do that?

The Calf: No, sir. I guess not.

The Chairman (to the secretary): Make a note of that, Miss Jersey. (To the calf) What's your excuse then, boy?

The Calf (scuffing a forehoof in the sand): Well, sir, I guess I don't have any real excuse. (Bravely) I just don't think it's fair, that's all. Why pick me? I just don't see any sense in it.

The Chairman (after a moment of stunned silence): No sense in it? Why, what if all young calves felt that way? Where do you think this country would be today?

The Old Angus (not unkindly): You don't want to betray the precious heritage of your forebulls, son. Think of all the brave young calves before you who have gladly made the supreme sacrifice for all that we cattle hold near and dear.

The Ancient Guernsey: Oh, how we wish we were still in our prime! Oh, what we'd give to be young enough to answer the call.

The Chairman (in fatherly fashion): That's right, son. We're bestowing on you the highest honor—the privilege of serving mankind and insuring the future of generations of cattle yet unborn.

The Calf (lifting his head): Yes, sir. Thank you, sir. I can see my duty clearly now. Which way do I go, sir?

The Chairman: Through that gate there, son, And don't be afraid. Remember, our prayers go with you.

The calf exits. (There is the beginning of a bleat cut off by a thud and followed by the sound of a falling body.)

The Secretary (her eyes moist): Oh, it tears at your heartstrings to see our brave young calves march off to do their duty.

The Chairman (briskly): Come, come, Miss Jersey. No time for emotionalism. We still need 13 more to meet our quota. Next, please.

To Root Against Your Country

The radio this morning said the Allied invasion of Laos had bogged down. Without thinking, I nodded and said, "Good."

And having said it, I realized the bitter truth: Now I root against my own country.

This is how far we have come in this hated and endless war. This is the nadir I have reached in this winter of my discontent. This is how close I border on treason:

Now I root against my own country.

How frighteningly sad this is. My generation was raised to love our country and we loved it unthinkingly. We licked Hitler and Tojo and Mussolini. Those were our shining hours. Those were our days of faith.

They were evil; we were good. They told lies; we spoke the truth. Our cause was just, our purposes noble, and in victory we were magnanimous. What a wonderful country we were! I loved it so.

But now, having descended down the torturous, lying, brutalizing years of this bloody war, I have come to the dank and lightless bottom of the well: I have come to root against the country that once I blindly loved.

I can rationalize it. I can say that if the invasion of Laos succeeds, the chimera of victory will dance once again before our eyes—leading us once again into more years of mindless slaughter. Thus, I can say, I hope the invasion fails.

But it is more than that. It is that I have come to hate my country's role in Vietnam.

I hate the massacres, the body counts, the free fire zones, the napalming of civilians, the poisoning of rice crops. I hate being part of My Lai. I hate the fact that we have now dropped more explosives on these scrawny Asian peasants than we did on all our enemies in World War II.

And I hate my leaders who, over the years, have conscripted our young men and sent them there to kill or be killed in a senseless cause simply because they can find no honorable way out—no honorable way out for them.

I don't root for the enemy. I doubt they are any better than we. I don't give a damn any more who wins the war. But because I hate what my country is doing in Vietnam, I emotionally and often irrationally hope that it fails.

It is a terrible thing to root against your own country. If I were alone, it wouldn't matter. But I don't think I am alone. I think many Americans must feel these same sickening emotions I feel. I think they share my guilt. I think they share my rage.

If this is true, we must end this war now—in defeat, if necessary. We must end it because all of Southeast Asia is not worth the hatred, shame, guilt and rage that is tearing Americans apart. We must end it not for those among our young who have come to hate America, but for those who somehow manage to love it still.

I doubt that I can ever again love my country in that unthinking way I did when I was young. Perhaps this is a good thing.

But I would hope the day will come when I can once again believe what my country says and once again approve of what it does. I want to have faith once again in the justness of my country's causes and the nobleness of its ideals.

What I want so very much is to be able once again to root for my own, my native land.

The Light Will Shine Again

The other day, in a sad and bitter mood, I wrote a column about how I had come to root against my own country in Vietnam because of this ugly, inane, interminable war.

I tried to say how it had been when I was young—how shining and noble and right my country had seemed to me. I tried to tell how this brutal, senseless war had tainted and degraded the love I had once felt for my own land. I tried to express the shame, the rage and the hopelessness that was in me.

There were depressing things to say, I said them because I thought they should be said. Then I waited for the mail to come in. I waited with dread.

In this business, you can usually predict the tone of the mail that any particular column will draw. I expected a few approving letters from the Left and a flood of hate mail from the Right. Those without strong views seldom bother to write a columnist.

The mail is coming in. And now I have something more to say because I think it should be said.

The first thing that surprised me about the mail was its volume. Never have I written a column that has attracted so many letters.

I opened the first few nervously. They were approving. The first dozen, the first score—all were approving. Of the first thousand, there were only twenty-four angry letters and most of those were unsigned.

Gradually, as I read through these letters agreeing with my stand and approving my expressing it, my spirits lifted.

Where I had been depressed, I was now elated. Where I had been sick and bitter, I was now proud.

Part of it, of course, was the approval. Every man cherishes approval. But it was more than that.

These letters were from people like me. A few, a very few, were from professional America haters. But the rest were from doctors, lawyers, accountants, housewives and one grand lady who typed under her signature, "A small, female and old voice from Santa Rosa."

Surprisingly many were from military men including four ex-Army Colonels. Surprisingly few were from college students. Most were of my generation, a probation officer, a policeman, a construction worker.

What they said, most of them, was that they, too, had seen their love for their country eroded by this endless war. And they, too, mourned it.

It was this, more than anything, that heartened me. In only a few societies could I have written what I wrote. In most, I would be clapped into jail. Yet these people, with nothing to gain, expressed their agreement and approval.

And they signed their names.

In this land, in these times, you can still stand up and say your country's wrong. More importantly, if you do, those who agree will stand up with you.

This, by God, is the greatness of this country.

This country is still sunk in the decaying mess that is Vietnam. We will be there, I think, for months or years to come. But my hopelessness has passed.

For even in that decaying mess, that which shone in my youth still glimmers. And now, for the first time in years, I believe with all my heart that it will shine again.

Mr. Hoppe
died on
February 4, 2000.

I sure admired him.
Reading Art Hoppe, Stanton Delaplane,
and Herb Caen in the
San Francisco Chronicles
in the 1960s and 1970s
sure brought solace AND fun
to me.

recent home visit to the

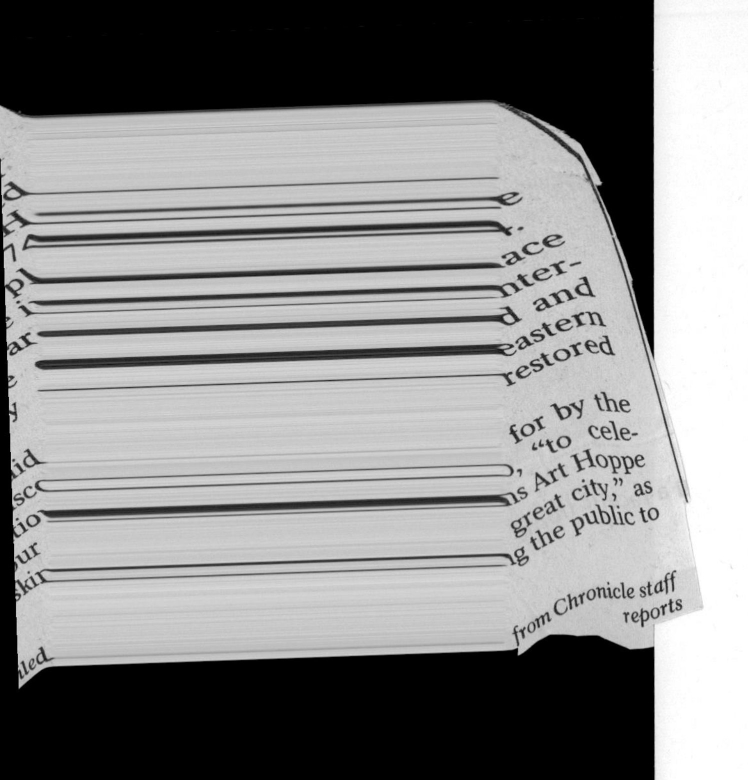

ace
nter-
d and
eastern
restored

for by the
, “to cele-
s Art Hoppe
great city,” as
g the public to

from Chronicle staff reports